Also by Ruby Gwin

The 250th Field Artillery Men Remember World War II

A Day That Would End Tearing at Your Heart

By Ruby Gwin

*We at Trafford believe that it is the responsibility of us all, as both individuals
and corporations, to make choices that are environmentally and socially sound.
You, in turn, are supporting this responsible conduct each time you purchase a
Trafford book, or make use of our publishing services. To find out how you are
helping, please visit www.trafford.com/responsiblepublishing.html*

*Our mission is to efficiently provide the world's finest, most comprehensive
book publishing service, enabling every author to experience success.
To find out how to publish your book, your way, and have it available
worldwide, visit us online at www.trafford.com*

 www.trafford.com

North America & international
toll-free: 1 888 232 4444 (USA & Canada)
phone: 250 383 6864 ♦ fax: 250 383 6804 ♦ email: info@trafford.com

To those who expressed their
solicitude during and throughout Dan's ordeal with much
support and prayers

Kudos to my wonderful
children, Deb, Wil, Melissa, Dan,
and Donya, from your loving
mother and mother-in-law.

INTRODUCTION

My hope is that you find Dan's story strengthening and inspiring. I have done my best to convey my thoughts and feelings as our family experienced them. From Dan, our family has learned firsthand the virtues of patience and wisdom. We have grown spiritually and taught that love and faith guides the way. It seems we live our lives in phases with there not being such a thing as typical.

Perhaps, Dan's story may not have ever been written had it not been for our son, Wil. When he would update the computer at the pharmacy he would have the old one refurbished for my use, which I eventually learned to put to good use.

To write an adequate account of events that cold, icy day 18 years ago wasn't easy. Although, I've reflected back on a day we will never forget. In life there is a mixture of tears and pain, Dan alone knows by accepting affliction one can be showered with HIS blessings.

Dan's response to his injury brings thoughts of how natural

it was for him as I had seen from my dear Mother. She was only five when her mother died with two small brothers. Her father wandered place-to-place after her mother died. Mother only vividly remembered her mother, my grandmother. Mother died almost 27 years ago. She never dwelled on her past or how hard and cruel life had been for her. She showered grace from under her inflicting early years of hardship as Dan has shown throughout his ordeal.

Believing will help create a deep courage of planning and striving with life. You will not see the shadow if you face toward the sunshine. God sometimes puts us on our backs so we may look upward.

One can learn to make the best of whatever by pursuing tasks just as Dan has chosen to do. It was with taking a personal journey in search of what he wanted for himself and found YOU HAVE TO BELIEVE. One of the hardest lessons we have to learn—there are no hopeless situations; believe that life is worth living and your belief will create the WAY.

God's Way

I knew our son would have a mission
  That he'd show us the way.

I knew not what God had in store
  I knew He'd guide the way.

I knew our son would look to Him above
  Who'd guide with love each step of the
  Way.

Ruby M. Gwin

~ CHAPTER 1 ~

THE WINGS OF PRAYER

$\mathcal{I}$t was a cold, icy February evening in 1988. A winter day that was to change our lives so drastically started like any other—just a normal day. I was preparing our evening dinner and my husband, Carl, had been at the farm and had just gotten in the house when the phone rang. Carl answered the telephone and was told that our son, Dan, had fallen and it didn't look good. Carl immediately rushed to Dan's place, just a quarter of a mile south of our house. He left leaving me unaware the seriousness of the fall. Dan had been cleaning the ice off the tarp of the trailer of his semi-trailer and lost his grip. He fell on the icy hard ground crushing his spine. While waiting it seemed like an eternity. Finally, Carl returned, he said, "An ambulance is taking Dan to the hospital." I found myself afraid from the expression on his face to ask, "How bad is it?" I was filled with fear for I knew his answer! We both just stood there not saying anything. I don't remember much from that point before our leaving for the hospital, I do remember calling our other son and daughter (both pharmacists) to tell them what I knew and where Dan was going to be taken.

Our drive to the hospital was so quiet. Thinking back—I can see myself so clearly that winter evening: a day that would end tearing at your heart. Thank God, the day could not be foreseen that morning. Sometimes we get pretty complacent in our thinking—taking everything-for-granted.

Once at the hospital, we waited around for sometime; finally, we were told by the neurosurgeon that nothing could be done, that Dan would be kept overnight and transferred the next day to a hospital in Indianapolis, Indiana. Carl and I both where exhausted, confused, and terribly frightened. Never had we ever felt so helpless. We felt Dan should have been lifelined *immediately* to the Trauma Center in Indianapolis, Indiana. Immediate medical care within the first 8 hours following injury is critical.

Carl was aware of the seriousness of the fall, for he was a medic during World War II. He tried to shield me by not saying anything, but I knew when I saw Dan at the hospital—no one had to tell me. Dan knew, too, for while waiting for the ambulance to arrive he said, "Dad, you will have to take care of things for me, I don't have any feeling in my legs." This I didn't know. I know this had to have been very hard on Carl for in so many ways he was helpless. The waiting for the ambulance had to be sheer terror for them both.

Carl and I lost track of time. We don't remember when we went home or our drive to the Methodist Hospital in Indianapolis—all is blank!

Late the next morning, Dan was transferred to the Methodist Hospital by ambulance where he lay in severe pain waiting to be taken care of in emergency. He had not been given anything for pain; they didn't want him to have anything until he had been seen by the neurosurgeon there. It was sometime before he was attended to in the emergency room and placed in the Spinal Cord Care Unit. It was evening before Dr. Feuer, a Neurosurgeon, came and talked with the family in a conference room. He said, "Your son is very smart, and he understands his condition is serious. There is a possibility you could lose Dan for the next three weeks. I will not operate right now; it may be a few days, for Dan could go into shock."

It was all so hard to comprehend, for everything had happened so fast. I could only find myself going from praying to asking, "Oh, God, why not me instead?"

It was so hard to stay calm, but I knew we all must to better help Dan, to keep him reassured for I knew he had to be frightened. We were frightened, too, for him. Yet, I realized that we should not let our fear of what might happen freeze us into inertia.

One morning in which I am not sure what day it was for everything was just reduced to begging from within for Dan to be alright, Carl and I came home to take care of some necessary business for Dan thinking it would be alright since they said they were going to wait to operate. There had been no mention of surgery yet. We made it as quick a trip as possible, but upon our arrival back at the hospital, we were told Dan had just been taken into the operating room. Words can never tell how we felt at that moment. I found myself in a trance; I felt so lost, hurt with an inability not wanting to believe what I heard. Carl nor I would have never left the hospital under any condition had we known. I do know though, Dr. Feuer felt Dan was stable enough for the surgery or he would not have proceeded. We felt the surgeons knew what they were doing and had made a right decision. Dr. Feuer would later become Dan's rock. He was the right doctor for Dan at the time. A wonderful man, a wonderful Neurosurgeon!

Hour after hour went by; it was a long ordeal where all your thoughts are on Dan. Finally, we were told Dan was in recovery and the Doctors would be out to talk with the family. My heart was pounding when Dr. Feuer, the first Doctor of the team came out. He said, "The surgery went well. When we operated the spinal cord went right back into place, thus, making it hopeful of a 50/50 chance of recovery, that it would be a while before we will know the results."

After the surgery, I got to go in to see Dan, but it will be an everlasting memory for me. At the first glance, it was not my son; I did not recognize Dan. It is forever framed in memory. He looked so swollen and shivering beyond belief in extreme cold. I believe he was packed in ice. They had his head in a downward position and one could see he was in serious condition.

There was a drug, Corticosteroids, at the previous hospital that could have been administered that would have taken down the swelling. I can't but wonder—had the swelling been relieved sooner *if* the outcome would have been a different story. The Neurosurgeon at the hospital felt that there was nothing could be done and said Dan would be transferred the next day to Indianapolis. It seems with some Doctors there is no in between—it is—or it isn't, but that is *not* always the case!

I am a firm believer there is always a hopeful chance of just maybe. It is a fact! The longer the swelling is on the spinal cord it causes the cells to die. As these cells die another wave of destruction radiates out from the damaged area. Dan should have been life-lined immediately to a Trauma Center. Prompt medical care by experts is a key factor in reducing permanent damage and disability resulting from spinal cord injury. Sparing further nerve damage is crucial. The cord is portion of the central nervous system enclosed in the vertebral column, consisting of nerve cells and bundles of nerves connecting all parts of the body with the brain. It contains a core of gray matter surrounded by white matter that is enveloped in three layers of membrane. There are 31 spinal nerves that leave the spinal cord and are distributed to the body and passing out from the vertebral canal through the spaces between the arches of the vertebrae. Each root has two roots—an anterior, carrying motor nerve fibers, and a posterior, carrying sensory fibers. Immediately after the roots leave the spinal cord they merge to form a mixed nerve on each side.

Dan's spinal cord had not been severed. Dan had a T10 lumber vertebra injury, which affects from the navel area down. The X-rays that were taken of Dan's spine were given to him. I never knew why they were given to Dan, but he still has them.

Shortly after surgery, I asked the orthopedic surgeon what Dan's chances for bladder and bowel control were and he just bluntly said, "He is paralyzed that is it!" There was *no* explaining anything. I felt at the time and I still do feel it was a cold hearted response. I had hoped he had had a hard day, but he never displayed any bedside manner throughout his caring for Dan. It was fine to be honest, but he could have been a little kinder with his response. Patients' worst enemy is passivity; lack of the normally expected type of response.

Dan's sister, Deb, brother, Wilson, and wife Melissa, a nurse, were all at Dan's bedside throughout the crisis; a family network of support is so important during such a crisis. We all stayed near by. During the first part of Dan's hospital stay, we stayed at an adjoining hotel where a skywalk would take you to and from the hospital. No one got much sleep. It was even hard to eat. Some of us stayed in the waiting room to be near Dan. As they say, you have to experience to understand. The uncertainty weighed heavily on us; we had no idea what was in store for Dan.

Dave Devitt, who had once rented the house where Dan now lives, was there with the family during the crisis. He is always there when called upon or in time of need. He has built a legacy of loyalty. His being there in our darkest times speaks for his character. Support network is so helpful at such a time. It was a time when new seeds of friendship are planted as well as faith. There were low points. As any parent, I didn't want Dan cheated out of that time in his life.

In the Intensive Care Unit, Dan had IVs, tubes and hoses just everywhere. It was difficult to go into ICU and see Dan lying there and unable to do anything for him. We were allowed to go in every hour for 5 minutes. I prayed for a source of strength to guide Dan throughout his ordeal. I could only watch and silently say, "God, please heal Dan, please." I knew it would be a miracle. I never ask why, but only ask for his help to guide and walk the road with our little boy.

Often the greatest source of strength during a difficult time is the feeling that we are not alone. During this time we received a very touching letter from our bank president's wife, Ellen Faust. Her words of faith; I cannot over emphasize what her inspiring words meant to Carl and I. One cannot know how essential it is to receive words of comfort at such a time. It was a letter written from the heart. That made the letter more meaningful—with it came some solace.

Everyone got their first glimmer of hope when the apparatus was starting to be removed and Dan was moved to a room. There were times that Dan was conscious to semiconscious—for brief periods. As I set at his bedside; I couldn't help but feel God had given our son to his father and I for the second time. The little boy that dragged a blue silk-type "blankie" around until it was nothing but a shabby threadbare piece of fabric. I went from fear to hope with a tremendous feeling of assurance—renewed strength of faith. Dan was heavily sedated on morphine. Morphine is a potent analgesic and narcotic that is used to relieve severe and persistent pain. It wasn't easy, for all we could do was watch over him and wipe his lips and mouth with swabs. Dan was zapped from the morphine and pain.

One day I was with our daughter at Dan's bedside when a nurse came in and gave him a shot in the stomach. Deb told her she never wanted to see that again because of the nerves in the stomach area. Deb is not a forceful person, but she was looking out for her brother. He had been given a type of shot that she knew could have been administered elsewhere than the stomach. There was some insensitive care shown in Dan's care. Where many of the hospital staff that worked with Dan was wonderful, others were thoughtless.

I felt like at times I was spinning around in a state of mental confusion. I started to ask myself, "How can Dan meet the challenges ahead and go on?" I soon learned it was by taking action to recover from his down fall. You do it step by step. I looked back on my childhood. I feel your own life history grows from that time; I wondered would I be as strong as Dan if I had encountered what my son, Dan, had? Our family doctor, Dr. Robert Leak, told Carl and I after the accident, that if Dan was a happy child it would make a difference on how he would cope. I felt if this is true—then, he would be alright, for he had been a happy, smiling child.

Dan still has that affective smiling expression. Dr. Leak's prophecy proved to be true. Thus, brought to memory, a day our Presbyterian minister came to the house to visit. Dan was playing on the floor with his road grader. Reverend John went over to where Dan was playing and asks him what he was doing. Dan looks up and replied, "Why, I am grading the road to church" as if Reverend John should have known what he was doing. Reverend John looked down at Dan and smiled, took his hand and ruffed Dan's hair, and called him "little minister". Dan was three years old. He was always busy with some type of toy equipment. Carl, Wil and Dan all have a John Deere toy collection.

~ CHAPTER 2 ~

HOMECOMING

*D*an had a T10 injury and paralyzed from the waist down. There was paralysis of all muscles below the level of injury, including those that control the bowel and bladder.

Dan graduated from Purdue University in 1981 receiving a Bachelor of Science degree in Agriculture Economics. He had just gotten a good start in farming—his dream. In a different position Dan now has to use his head as never before. He has never complained that his injury robbed him or that he would be on medication daily or in a wheelchair permanently. He has been an inspiration for the whole family, as well as others. Dan has taught us all no matter how something may seem or be it is the positive attitude and faith that counts! He endures each new day with a bright smile and hopeful gleam in his eyes.

Dan was told he would be in the hospital for 4-6 months. He made a bet with Dr. Feuer that he would be out sooner—he was out in 5 weeks. We were amazed to see this new courage. I knew Dan wasn't alone, for he had what his one handicap detour would be, *faith.*

I was deeply moved by the way Dr. Feuer cared for Dan. He told Dan to ask for the food the race car drivers got. In doing so, the dietitian acted like she didn't know what he was talking about until Dan told her Dr. Feuer told him to ask for it. He got the food.

The Methodist Hospital is known to be one of the best places to go for spinal cord injuries. Their trauma center is equipped to handle such injures. At that time there was a special suite for the race car drivers. They had their own kitchenette and had special chefs. Now there is a special room for the race car drivers on each floor of the hospital where different types of injuries are cared for. The Methodist Hospital handles a lot of the race car drivers' injuries. I wonder, though, about the innocent victims that had nothing to do with what happened to them—should they be treated differently?

Dan had to have intensive rehab before coming home. There were a series of things he had to do: had to learn to dress himself, balance himself, to transfer from bed to wheelchair, wheelchair to car seat, jump curbs and learn to care for himself and how to prevent pressure sores. A paralytic has a lot to endure. The occupational therapists start the process of rehabilitation. They soon learn to make use of the strength left in their muscles. During their rehab process they learn they will have to spend a lot of time just caring for their own needs.

Dan's day of homecoming I felt frightened at first, for I feared he would hurt himself. That fright turned to a feeling that he would manage. He had shown everyone it was not a dead-end. He assured us with his enthusiastic determination; I couldn't help but feel he would succeed—that being his fathers and my comfort. We felt part of a great burden had been lifted. Dan had gone through a lot but wasted no time working on where he is today. He learned it is so important to know the details of your own care and because there are so many things about the body functions and problems that call for knowing and discipline.

Being paralyzed there are things that can develop and you don't always know when something is wrong. One's daily life is changed drastically with lasting effects. Modifications are necessary for a person with a spinal cord injury in their home. A vocational rehabilitation is most important to help restoring the independence after an injury. Dan traveled to Indianapolis three times a week for two years for physical therapy; each session personally paid up-front cost $55.00. I then, started doing his leg exercises, which allowed him to maintain the strength and mass of his leg muscles. I was motivated to keep up his exercises for nerves can find new pathways. It helped that Dan maintained a positive attitude by being highly motivated and patient. It certainly calls for a patient to take the needed steps upfront, because of the caring process ahead.

Dan had to lean on others to get things done after he returned home. For the most part things went pretty well. There was one young boy; Matt Clouser that helped Dan. He has a brother that has Multiple Sclerosis that he helped his parents with. Matt was good help. He would take control and would see things got done. Matt instinctively knew when to help Dan and when not to, because of his experience with his brother, Luke. Dan would use his leg braces and with Matt holding him firmly would try to walk. Dan had been taught to shift his body side-to-side. Dan never tries it anymore other than occasionally he will stand up at the kitchen sink or walk alongside of his pickup. Matt not only would look out for Dan, but after Carl's Aortic Valve implant would make sure Carl got up into the large 4-wheel tractors. Matt, a thoughtful young man, will always be special to Dan and our family. He occasionally will stop and visit with Dan. His little boy likes to ride the tractor or combine with Dan.

Not only young, Matt Clouser and David Devitt were so dear to our family during this time. There was C.K. Wilkins, a young fellow that loves the land as much as Dan. He was there for Dan,

Carl and I when we needed a strong hand. For me, he is extra special: he helped Dan with the planting, Carl when he needed help, as well as being my rock during those dark days. It makes me remember—not everything is transitory in life, for we were shown it is most promising.

Dan wore a chest brace when he came home for 6 months. It was just like a cast that hugged his upper body. It immobilized his body while healing. Dan was sure happy when he no longer had to wear it, for it was hot and heavy to wear. It was summer time, which made it more uncomfortable and caused sweating. It also was easier afterward to move around without it.

The one thing that was noticeable was occasionally someone had to lift Dan up while he was in the wheelchair. He was more comfortable with some lifting him than others. Sometimes he seemed a little frightened. Matt was the one that he felt comfortable with. With Matt's brother in a wheelchair he was used to handling one. Dan has fallen from the wheelchair and had to climb back up into it on his own.

The spinal cord responses with an injury can be unpredictable. There are people that have had a dramatic response in their paralysis after a few years. Where it can happen for one person it won't another. One has to be realistic and move on preparing for the worst then you won't be disappointed; exiting or occurring in reality, but keep ones faith. A paralytic always has hope of one day walking.

An Orthopedic Surgeon told Carl and I about an Indianapolis doctor that was in an automobile accident and had incurred the same injury as Dan. He said, "The hole in the vertebrae where the spinal cord is was large and that his damage to the spinal cord was only temporary. He had received care immediately at the Trauma Center." Time *is* of the essence in a spinal cord injury. I am sure this all played a major role in his recovery.

Dan was weight lifting before his injury, building his upper torso; he had become very muscular. It helped for the extensive rehab that he had to go through. Dan had to modify his home and farm operation in order to better accommodate his disability.

At first, one would have thought his biggest challenge he had to face was psychological, but that never seemed to be the case. Dan had self esteem with a belief in tomorrow that provided him with security—a sense of purpose! For others, there had to be skepticism, without lack of experience with an injury as Dan's. Dan had been where some of us never had been; everything was dark, except, Dan could see the light. It was a very, very bright light with a firm conviction of believing. He had confidence he would do things he once had—just doing them differently. His optimism about things has always been good; optimism is a kind of a heart stimulant. Dan is very fortunate because he has the skill to make things happen in a way that benefits him. Each day he has his routine that takes self-discipline, which he is in the position of controlling. In his darkest experiences, he started to look for optimism and affirmation is how he built new self-esteem and redirected his energy to the light. It has been an extraordinary adventure; one can only be struck with awe when one sees Dan's optimism at work.

Instead of staying in out of reach, it was Dan that did the reaching; which was no surprise. He realized it takes discipline, tenacity, and hard work to find your life's work, in that, reaching out was one of those steps. He knew the seeds of hope must be planted in the soil of opportunity and cultivated with a personal commitment to place his dream within the grasp to reach for it. Knowing hope alone would not achieve his dream, but reaching out would. Dan knew no one's ever been successful without having a goal—and a plan for how to achieve it. He knew it was up to him to make his dream work, which gave him the confidence, which gave him the inner strength to reach out to believe in knowing he could make it.

Hope is not confined, but only means one changing their priorities just enough to keep the doors of opportunity open. Hope for Dan was the harvest of *both* goal and investment ... a vision ahead meant a lot of striving with enduring faith that the horizon of possibilities *are* limitless.

I believe to cultivate hope, to make it come true, to place it within grasp, we must ideology own an ideal of believing. I feel one can chose his way by taking a directorate action seeking to achieve an effective means by proceeding from one point to another. In some things, we have to be patient oriented. One doesn't want to dwell on what is at the end of the track but what is at the front and ride the way to the final destination. There are many stops along the way, but enjoy each stop and go on. One's own journey is what he makes it. Carl and I have seen a lot of incredible things happen; faith and love are most important. Many years ago on TV, I heard a poem: The End of the Road is but a Bend in the Road. I don't remember how it went. It was written by Helen Steiner Rice. I do remember part of it, "Let go and let God share your load, your work is not finished or ended" and "You've just come to a bend in the road". This verse stuck with me through the years. The bend is only as short as one makes it. Dan can attest to that!

For me, I sometimes would go a long way down the road in a quandary, suffering from within. I was deeply worried as any parent would be. Carl and I spent hours pleading to up above. It was the quiet times that were the worst. Gone was the gaiety that always was a part of our life. I look back and realize I lived in the moment for three-four weeks—not knowing where the road would take us. It was Dan that showed the way by taking the high road. When a child hurts—parents hurt too. It was an unexplainable hurt.

Dan wearing the shirt I made for him

This is the last family picture that was taken before Dan's injury. Back L-R: Melissa, Wil's wife, Wil, Ruby, Carl, Dan and Deb sitting in front

Dan is preparing his "Christmas Sweepstakes" for Mom & Dad

Above: Dan looks out at the sun going down, just as he will be up to see it come up. Below: Channel 8 (CBS), Ken Owens, outreach coordinator, Gary Stoops of "Breaking New Ground Resource Center" at Purdue University and Dan.

Dan is transferring from wheelchair to lift to get up into the tractor with the use of braces.

Dan is using the lift to raise himself up to transfer over into the tractor seat.

Matt Clouser is showing his two 4-H pigs at the Montgomery County fair grounds.

~ CHAPTER 3 ~

INCOMPREHENSIBLE MIRACLES

*T*he year 1989 was a long year, and then Carl found stair steps and walking was starting to bother him. When he went to our family doctor, Dr. Leak, for a checkup he told Carl he thought it was his heart and said, "As soon as you get the harvesting done that you should have it checked." It had only been a few months since Carl had an EKG, which showed everything was okay. After harvest, we made an appointment at the St. Vincent Hospital in Indianapolis, Indiana. It was where Melissa guided us to go. At the time, she worked as a nurse on ICU's cardiac floor at the IU Medical Center. St. Vincent Hospital is known to be one of the leading heart disease facilities in the nation. They do all types of coronary artery bypass surgeries, cardiac operations and valvular operations. The Cardiologist there did a catheterization and found Carl needed immediate attention. The test revealed Carl needed an aortic valve replacement and was told if he chose to go home he'd have to stay on the sofa. It was Christmas time, but Carl chose to stay and have the surgery.

This time it wasn't icy weather, but snow. I went home and got the car stuck in the drive way as I was leaving to return to the hospital, over an hour away. I said, "God, please help me get out for I need to get back to the hospital." I sat there in the car for a few minutes before making another attempt to get out; finally, I was able to get enough moving power employed for movement. I didn't want to bury it deeper or hurt the transmission trying to get out. There were two different neighbors that came while I was at the hospital and cleared the drive way. I found they are there with divine assistance in time of need.

Doctors replaced the aortic valve with a mechanical valve and did two by-passes. Carl was under the care of his anesthesiologist for 48 hours. I stayed near by and had gone to look through the window the first night and I saw something was wrong. A nurse saw me standing at the window and came and told me what had happened. She let me in to see Carl. He had started to bleed and had to have blood transfusions. It was quite emotional time for all of us for Carl had a few setbacks and was slow to recover. It required a longer time for his progress and his hospital stay was longer than normal. He was to have therapy before he was discharged, but he never gained the strength.

This time, with his family, Dan was there waiting for results of his father's surgery. Meanwhile, Dan had been transferring from wheelchair to a sofa to rest. In doing so he must have bruised his leg for he got a blood clot. Deb had to stay with him for there was no way I could have taken care of him. She helped me so much.

It was a particularly tiring and trying time. I was weary and tired. I couldn't rest at night. I stayed close to Carl at the hospital. Carl and Dan both finally got better. After Carl got home he faithfully exercised; the key to his regaining his strength. He was able to do the corn and soybean planting in the spring.

With mechanical valves you need to take anti-coagulant

medication to prevent blood clots from forming around the new valve. It was hard to get the Coumadin adjusted with Carl. It got where Carl had to go every two weeks to get his blood drawn; he always had a bruised arm.

Carl or Dan both never experienced depression for they understood what was ahead for each and chose to meet the facts head-on. The saying is—you can take the boy from the country, but you can't take the country out of the boy!

Dan had started working from his hospital bed taking care of business matters. It would be harvest time before Dan was able to do any field work. He was pushing himself, but he was anxious. Within days, we began to see a change in Dan as he got back into the combine, new energy seemed to flow. I feel this may have been the answer to his injury acceptance. He kept his mind occupied for he was determined to get back to doing what he had been doing. He was concerned how the landlords that he farmed for would react, but each stood beside him and gave him a chance to see what he could do. Once again he not only proved to himself, but they saw the determination that he had. He proceeded from his natural "Self-Acting" characteristic—his love for farming had a lot to do with it. He has a special relationship with all his landlords. Each one has a special quality that Dan shall never forget. They each have been steadfast in their support of Dan to which there has never been an unwavering course. Dan feels close to each one—like family.

His father's semi-retirement in 1988 increased Dan's acres and made better usage of equipment and increased his income. It made Dan more independent to self-governing the farm operation by incorporating his own ideas.

~ Chapter 4 ~

Blessings

*I*n 1995 Dan was chosen by the Montgomery County Jaycee's "Farmer of the Year" as well as representing Indiana in the US Junior Chamber of Commerce, the Jaycee's "Outstanding Young Farmer Award Congress of the year". Carl and I got to go with Dan to Bakersfield, CA for the National State Farmer award. The award ceremony was to have been at Kobe, Japan, site, but they had endured a devastating earthquake.

Dan never won the National award, but the trip and getting to meet the 26 "State's Farmer of the Year" was so enjoyable. We had a good time. We have many pictures of the event. Dan prayed he wouldn't get the national award, for he felt it would be said he got it due to his being in the wheelchair. He withheld information that would have helped him, but it went the way he wanted it to go. With his parents teaching of common goals and values and within that framework, Dan had a broad freedom to make his own decisions.

It was his call to do it his way–we were so proud of him!

During the time we were there, we got to take a bus tour and saw the Bakersfield farming area, and we went through some factories. It was educational and interesting. What was interesting was the history about carrots. When carrots were first cultivated in central Asia, the most common varieties were green and purple. Can one imagine! They were not used as a food, but as a medicine. The Arabian traders in the Twelfth century brought the cultivated carrot to the Mediterranean area. By the Eighteenth Century, the growers developed a wide variety with the appearance of the orange carrot that we enjoy today. What is interesting is some of the fashion-mindful women used the feathery leaf top to decorate their hair, and in Germany, a hot beverage was made from carrots which had been chopped into small pieces and roasted. They have become primarily for the use in cooking. It was discovered that by removing the leafy top, carrots stayed moist for a longer time—a discovery which improved both quality and the shelflife of carrots. We got to see how they were handled for preserving. Now the under size carrots are used for fresh peeled baby carrots; used as a quick snack or for hors d'oeuvres. We were shown how they were washed and stored in large grain bins. The storage was large bins we use for corn and soybeans. It was interesting how the carrots were preserved for future use.

The much used carrots are a good source of vitamin A. Carrots are nutritious, and the vitamin A is suppose to fight cancer, good for eye vision, cell production and helps to guard against bacterial infection.

We met Ralph Thompson who had a garlic (Ralph and Leo) farm that we toured that was interesting. Ralph had been here at Purdue and familiar with the area—interesting man! A young fellow, Dan Hernstedt that was very active with the *Friends of Agriculture* had an orange orchard in Bakersfield. He invited Dan to come back for a visit. He said, "I have a huge house that you can stay at one end and we'll stay at the other end." The two Dan's seem to have a lot in common to talk about. Dan and his wife, Christine, were on the NOYF Host Committee. Dan had talked he'd like to go visit them, but it never worked out. They were an impressive unpretentious couple.

It was a wonderful tour that ended with a luncheon at the Tejon Ranch. We saw a lot of irrigation on our scenic tour after our lunch. On the hillsides you could see the pipes where water was being piped in. While on the scenic tour, we were entertained by Ronny Lee who liked to have fun. He was an outstanding young farmer from New Jersey that never missed an opportune moment to talk with an ability to evoke laughter with his playful wit.

One of the six NOTY judges, Mr. Carrigan, (President of Outstanding farmers of America) was on the bus tour. When they were getting Dan out at the carrot farm I heard him make a remark about having to bother with Dan. It really hurt! His wife saw that I heard him and came over to talk with me. My eyes began to burn and I knew I was about to cry. I felt sorry for her as well as my son, Dan. She tried to be friendly. I thought it was nice of her, but I really needed to be by myself for a few minutes. It was hard to hold the tears back. Dan never knew it took place.

Mr. Carrigan had been an "Outstanding Young Farmer of America" himself. He farmed 100 acres of retail marketing in North Carolina. He had not been helping Dan. There were many fellas willing to help Dan as well as the bus driver. I don't know what the problem was unless he felt Dan hadn't been a good candidate being in a wheelchair. Dan wasn't slowing up the tour. When we got to the ranch, they were not waiting on us and other buses were just arriving. They had a luncheon, but I wasn't able to eat much. The thoughts were just too painful. I told Carl that night what occurred for I wanted him to be sure to help watch out for Dan's interest.

I feel especially sympathetic to those that are in their own little world. To me, the essential thing for Dan fundamentally is not to let those types bother him. It is important in his daily life and actions. It has taken courage to choose the road less traveled. One can only feel sorry for those that are so wrapped in their own self that they don't want to be bothered with anyone or anything that may take a few minutes longer. Each day the handicap meets the stereotype that represents a prejudiced attitude that the handicap has no place in a certain type of environment. I pray that Mr. Carrigan, or perhaps a love one, never has to encounter what Dan has, for life can change for anyone in a few seconds. People need to remember Dan *is* still Dan. One soon learns that there are people that aren't sympathetic of others' distress or a desire to help alleviate distressing circumstances affecting an individual. One learns fast— you win some, you lose some! Dan learned early after his injury to look beyond and move on to *His* goal! There wasn't time to waste on what people thought.

Dan came out a winner—he got to meet some wonderful young farmers that he would have never met otherwise. Dan had been chosen to represent the state of Indiana by the United States Junior Chamber of Commerce (Jaycees); paying tribute to our young men in agriculture.

A couple, Danny and Sandra Wilkerson, from Kentucky sent Dan some pictures that they had me to take of them with Dan at the airport. We were all homeward bound. Dan was happy to get the pictures—so thoughtful. Lindsey Larson and wife, Debra, (winner) stayed with us as long as they could on our trip back. We parted at the Texas airport. They were nice. Dan also met Michael and Carol Deavers from Kansas, Jeff and Jan Topp from North Dakota (winner) that he thought a lot of.

There was a lady that was really outstanding in what she had done after her husband suddenly passed away. She was a young mother that had been helping operate 1,290-acres in Minnesota. Financial hardship sat in and her father-in-law had to have heart surgery, she hung in there making it in the male-dominated industry. Tammy Hildebrandt-Haley to me was a winner; her determination was an act of gallantry. I truly admired her for the personal courage of carrying on a mission—what an achievement! Part of coping with stress is maintaining a sense of perspective. This is the type of stories we need to hear rather than so much negative.

Everyone was nice. I felt any one could have been chosen. It was really hard to single out any one couple. I would not have wanted the job of choosing. We enjoyed ourselves and were so thankful that we got to share it with Dan—much thanks to the Indiana Jaycees.

It would have been nice to have seen more of Bakersfield while we were there, but with the time schedules there just wasn't enough time. Bakersfield lies in the southern San Joaquin Valley. The area is a big patchwork of fields and orchards that spread north toward central California and south toward the Tehachapi range separating the city from the Mojave Desert and the Los Angeles basin. Sierra Nevada east of Bakersfield rises to a wall-like ridge while the coast range west forms a washboard of steepening hills that extends to the Pacific Ocean.

Bakersfield's traditionally known for oil and cotton, which continues to thrive, but there has been the rise of their growing fruits, vegetables, almonds, pistachios. Sheep and cattle also constitute an agriculture landscape. Oil boomed after the discovery of the Kern River field in 1899 where 67% of the states and 9% of the nation's petroleum out-put comes from the area. Kern County also provides 41% of California's natural gas. Their oil leads agriculture in total worth. Cotton has long been the county's top crop.

Bakersfield we found quite different from our Indiana "Amber Waves of Grain" where farmers grow large fields of corn, soybeans and wheat. We live in Montgomery County, which in 2006 was the fourth largest producer of corn in the state, producing 844.7 million bushels and ranked first in soybeans. We use to raise more corn than beans until Carl and Dan changed to a crop-rotation pattern. Some of the counties that rank higher in corn have more farm acres.

While in Bakersfield, we stayed at the Red Lion Inn. It was very nice. It had a nice ballroom where the Mexican Fiesta Reception and Banquet, luncheons, and awards ceremony were held. Next after the California visit, Dan was due in Louisville, Ky., to do a slide presentation for the National Farm Machine Show. The time all went fast; soon Dan was back to being busy at the farm where his Bakersfield trip would fade to a pleasant memory.

1995 Outstanding State Young Farmer

Above: The "National Outstanding Young Farmer Awards Congress" group from 26 states. Below: Breakfast before departure for home. Left front: Dan, Ruby and Carl.

L-R: Sandra & Danny Wilkerson, from Kentucky, and Dan at the Los Angeles Airport—homeward bound.

~ Chapter 5 ~

Life's Golden Gift of Wisdom

——————

*W*hen Carl farmed, he always looked forward to autumn; it was the time to harvest the fruits he had worked the long hours in the spring for. I, myself, always looked forward to the arrival of spring. A time that is the spiritual rebirth of things we hold dear. I am always uplifted with seeing the greening of God's creation. Like an Emerald, it's green likened to the cool verdure of the earth, to me meant tranquility. For Carl it always meant taking to the field soon. I would prefer everything stayed green, but that wouldn't be very profitable.

Farming has changed. It has become a large business requiring good management. The bad farmers were weeded out in the '80s when a farmer was taught to be more debt cautious & efficient— emphases were on profit, not production. The Bakersfield, CA trip introduced us to the different aspects of farming. We got to see a highly diversified agricultural community in Kern County where they produced over 1.9 billion worth of agricultural commodities for the retail market at that time in 1995. We were exposed to a different aspect of farming than what I had known growing up.

Farmers and researchers work to develop and test cutting edge technologies. Dan uses GPS (Global Positioning System) mapping techniques that help him by correlating both the yield and nutrient sets of data, farmers can determine very specifically what nutrient content produces the best yields at any given location and then apply additional nutrients to those specific areas as exactly as needed. It is a more cost efficient way to fertilize—applying just where and what is needed. It has been very beneficial in Dan's operation. Yield monitors and soil sensors produce a lot of data.

Dan has satellite auto power systems that guides his tractors and combine. How it performs is so amazing. He can eat while the machine will guide itself across the field. The electronics revolution with accompanying development of the satellite and the computer technology has revolutionized education for a lifetime—rather than a once-in-a-life time.

Farmers are using the technology now more out of farming intuition than out of information based on research. Global Positioning System using satellites was created to assist our military navigation; civilian use includes tracking aircraft, ships and motorists. A creation now farmers are benefiting from and so thankful for.

When Dan returned to the farm after he graduated, he wanted to implement the management that he was taught at Purdue. He had to learn that farm operations are different. Although, taught well—he had to learn to put what he was taught into perspective. He had to learn the capacity to view things in their true relations in a larger framework. He was learning this when he was injured. He is a good farmer as well as manager. He was taught well for his father also was a good steward of the ground. Wil and Dan have benefited from those early years of their father's indoctrinate.

The Farming heritage runs deep in the heart of the Gwin

family. Dan will be the last with the Gwin name to farm to any degree, for he has no children. I don't know of any other that has any attachment to the farm that has the means to farm other than for Carl's nephew, Brad. Brad does some small scale farming, but at one time, that was all he did. Brad has retired from his city police job, and has returned to his grass roots of farming. They still have a part of the farm that Brad learned to farm on with his parent's, Bill and Mary Gwin.

Son, Wilson, has a very deep love of the farm, but with him being a pharmacist, returning to the farm is very remote. Times change, and farming will go on. There will be others to follow to continue to shape what will become theirs as those before them.

Dan does all the planting, spraying and combining himself. He has hired help to fill the planter and sprayer. He unloads into semi-trucks that are driven by hired help. His main help is a fella along with part time help; some are students at Purdue that work part time. They are farm boys themselves. It helps that Dan lives close enough to Purdue University for the students to help out. Like Dan they, too, want to farm. Many won't be able to return to the farm in the midst of despair and uncertainty. Farms are getting not only large but Hi-Tech. Many students are choosing career paths that allow them to stay connected to agriculture. Many are working in marketing, sales, packing, and food sciences, while students' studying traditional areas like agronomy is decreasing. Dan had three young boys, Clint Arnholt, Matt Hartman and Jason Carnahan that would come out and work on the farm while they were going to Purdue.

Matt and Jason still come to help out when time allows. Clint use to come, but now is involved full time on the family farm that his mother had been personally operating. Matt is a manager of a large grain facility, but still helps whenever time permits. Jason returned to the family dairy and grain farm after graduation. All doers—they enjoyed coming and helping Dan. All three had been well coached on the farms where they grew up. Working for Dan was just an ordinary job to them—touch of home!

I grew up in the rural area. There was never an adjustment for me to live on the farm. I like being outdoors. We always had a large garden and mother did a lot of canning. We children always enjoyed roaming the fields, climbing trees, wading in the creeks, picking violets and dandelions in the woods for our mother to put in her bottle neck jar with water.

I can understand the young men wanting to return to the farm for it is a good life. They are their own boss, but they still have the responsibility of the management, which takes much forethought. Farming is a gamble and at times not very profitable; income depends a lot on Mother Nature and the price of grain. Our forefathers had this special pride: after a crop disaster, they'd start looking forward to a new spring with a spirit that it would awaken what autumn puts to sleep.

Today, the farm environment is *such* that all aspects have to be looked at differently than from yesteryears' farming. Speculating is one thing, serious farming is something else. Farmers no longer can farm small as they once did without an additional income.

Carl was a farm boy and would have to get up early to do chores before going to school. Carl did different types of work, but farming was always his passion. The time he served in the army during World War II and when he went to Purdue University are the only times he wasn't connected to the farm in some way. It was a way of life that he would hold dear.

The inputs and the equipment has gotten so expensive and the cash rent have gotten so high where a young person cannot start farming without money back of them or there is room on the farm for them to return. There aren't near as many farms today as there was when I was growing up. Many of the rural areas where farms used to be have become housing divisions. The demand for land has made the farm ground more expensive to purchase, for some too prohibitive.

Today, farmers have to travel a further distance if they want something. It used to be if Carl needed some nails, nuts or bolts he could go locally to purchase them. That was the good old days—now it is 12 miles or more.

With farming there are always tasks to do. There is a tradition that is all but gone today—neighbors helping each other to help ease the burden. It would be hard to provide children today a window to yesteryear, for it would show the simplicities and harsh difficulties of a life they would never know. I don't believe some would be able to adapt after being exposed to the environment as they know it today.

With the legacy history we are passing on, we hope one day our grandchildren will want to know more about their family roots, finding some guidance in the old traditions. For our family, our love of the farm served to steer us through difficult times. Our children today don't have any comprehension what our forefathers did to make the farming what it is today. They worked long hours with a team of mules that they drove in front of the planter. As Carl said, "Nostalgia is definitely the best part of the experience."

Carl's father planted 10 acres a day, shelled seed corn by hand that had been wire check-row planted; using a wire stretched from one end of the field to the other end of field with knots every 36 inches where the seed was to be dropped. At the end of the row they'd pull the wire just enough to raise two or three buttons in front of the horses; hold the wire exactly so every time until the pin was started into the ground and the rows would be reasonably straight cross way. The planter would drop a kernel at each knot planting two rows at a time. Check row planter would plant the cross straight if properly handled. Cross cultivating was the farmers' only means to control weeds. There was no urging the team, for every time they were made to go a little faster the hills would be out of line. The yield was around fifty bushels an acre using no fertilizer. It was a nuisance to contend with the check-row, and there were countless efforts for years to perfect a wireless way of planting. The check-row system was the most widely way to plant corn. It was during World

War II that Carl's father changed from check-row planting and the use of horses to planting with a tractor.

Carl came home from service to a big change. One could say— Hi-Tech! Carl missed out on the joy of getting to see the arrival of a 4-row planter and tractor after having driven mules for so long. He has his father's first tractor that was purchased new as Dan has our first new tractor. It is a 3020 with a loader. It is now an antique used around the farm, which brings happy memories when seen performing its many different duties.

Carl's father, Earl, check-row planting '1935

Today Dan plants with the same manpower 200 acres a day with a high yield return on corn. He plants with a 16 row planter using fertilizer and insecticide while planting. The tractors today are designed where Dan can use hand controls. He uses levers that he has made himself for the clutch and brake pedal. He makes things work for him to get the job done.

Dan has protected who he is by choosing to overcome setbacks and work through objections. He listens and has learned to be open to constructive ideas. He does a lot of forethought to making decisions. He will even call and ask me certain things—this makes me proud that he feels that I may have the knowledge to help with a decision. He has demonstrated that he can stick to his principles and to be able to act on them. He has the ability and work ethic to be successful in a business where he has learned that there is so much volatility; subject to rapid or unexpected changes. There is some sort of agriculture calamity every year, but it doesn't veer Dan away from the farm environment. The next year it is Déjù vu all over again.

Today, it takes a lot of pencil pushing to stay on top in farming. If you don't care for calculating figures—farming is not the best choice. It takes meticulous work to be successful. People don't realize what goes on to feed our country. Farmers, in effort, are the foot soldiers in the front lines of America. Our farmers feed the world.

Carl's exposing the boys early on has been beneficial to them both in countless ways. They were taught a good work ethic; dealing with what is good and bad. Carl and I tried to guide each child with good moral principles of duty and obligation knowing a person does not succeed in everything; you never will, but a person should never stop attempting to succeed. Life is what each makes it … hand in hand we live and learn with a pursuit of wisdom.

~ CHAPTER 6 ~

GREATEST TIMES

$\mathcal{S}$ome of our greatest times were when the children were growing up. Parenting is not only a challenge but a unique experience that is sometimes difficult. One never thinks that one day just a few seconds would change things forever; it happens so quickly. Both of the boys learned to farm at a very young age. I would stand at the door concerned with them on the tractor until one day, Carl said, "Mother, let go!"

Mothers don't let go like fathers, but I did. I decided to be proud of what they were learning rather than stand at the door fearing the worst. I learned they were having fun while Mother was worrying—this gave me comfort. I no longer stood at the door watching for that "something" to happen.

Reflecting back on when the children were small one takes everything for granted not thinking of what may lay in store. It is a blessing one cannot foresee the future. It is essential for everyone to stay focused when a family faces such a drama.

Our children were always close. When something was done and the boys were asked *who* did it, both would take the blame covering for the other. They dearly loved teasing big sister. She never did tell on them. When Dan was corrected he'd invariably run to Deb. She was his protector—he thought! Dan was the hardest to discipline for he would test you where Wil or Deb wouldn't. It was hard to keep a straight face for he'd do things to make you laugh—still does! Children are different and have to be handled differently.

Mothers want to shield their children. I know I did. What Carl said on that early morning some years ago helped me to let go. I grew myself from that moment. The one thing you don't want to do is not clip their wings too soon but, they need to learn to stand up for themselves. It use to be mothers were the one that spent the most time with the children, and I found as a mother I had to become a leader and trainer. It is a unique time for values, leadership and character of a child. It takes a lot of work, care and most of all love. I was the main discipliner, yet, I worked at not only telling but showing them love.

I was brought up not in money, but we children had a wealth of love and faith our Mother gave so lovingly. I don't remember my mother raising her voice or spanking any of us children. Prayer begins where human capacity ends. The strength my mother gave helped me to endure what sometimes seems to be the impossible. I focused from my own childhood to help guide our children to work toward advancing their own vision. Carl and I worked at giving our children a strong foundation. We taught each to work. We never traveled much, but when all three graduated from Purdue University the same year we took them to Hawaii for 10 days. We had a good time, a lasting memory for each. It was the last trip the whole family would make together.

We went to the four islands. We spent New Years in 1979 on Maui. The next day there was an inch of firecrackers on the ground. One would have thought it was 4th of July! One night, Deb and the boys went out where there was dancing. The boys didn't want Deb to sit with them so the girls wouldn't think she was a date. Deb said, "I went and sat at another table alone. I don't know if it helped the boys with the girls or not...."

There was another dear couple, Russel and Tillie Miller that went with us to Hawaii. We stayed at the Waikiki Beach-Comber Hotel while on Honolulu. Don Ho, a Waikiki icon, wearing a bright Hawaiian shirt and white slacks would sing in the evening and couples could dance. One evening, Russel ordered him and Carl a Mai Tai. With it being "Happy Hour" the drinks were doubled. Carl didn't drink his, so Russel drank all four along with eating hot peppers with his dinner. Boy! It was funny; I was convulsed with laughter. His wife, Tillie, said she had never seen me laugh so hard. Russel was not use to drinking. He was funny during the evening, but didn't feel so good the next day. He was pretty quiet ... I think he was embarrassed. I didn't see him drank anymore "Mai Tai" drinks. It certainly was a memorable evening!

One evening all of us were setting around a table talking when a nice looking young fella came up and asked me, "Would you like to dance?"

I replied, "No, thanks, but my daughter would."

Tillie never got over telling that story. Oh, what fun we had! Tillie was a cousin of a teacher that I had, Mr. Lindley. While attending Purdue University, Deb lived in the same dormitory as Mr. Lindley's daughter, Betty. The two girls became very close. Deb was one of Betty's bridesmaids when she got married.

Hawaii is just a group of islands with much to see. We took a tour of the countryside. The scenery was very relaxing on the Kona coastline where we took the Captain Cook Cruise. On Honolulu we visited the Punchbowl Pearl Harbor National Cemetery where we took a tour aboard the "Leilani" boat at Waikiki. A World War II veteran's memorial sight—a beautiful view site; yet sad! Thousands of our men lost their lives on that early Sunday morning of December 7, 1941 surprise attack on our U.S. Naval

Base on Honolulu, Hawaii.

We saw beautiful Hibiscus, the red Hibiscus is the state flower, Hawaii Volcano National Park area, beautiful Japanese gardens and banana trees.

At the Hilo Greenhouse, we saw colorful orchids growing on trees, beautiful anthodium's, papaya trees and a coconut plantation. On Kona, there was a luau where they roasted a pig underground, and we were entertained by the Hawaiian hula dancers. It was a fun evening. At "La-Hainu," Maui there was an Indian Banyan Tree, oldest in the islands that spread 175 feet. Everyone took a cruise to Fern Grotto up the Wailua River where there was an evergreen cave at Kauai where couples went to get married. On Kauai the rain was called "pineapple juice" for it was kind of like a light spray—very beautiful!

Maui was our favorite island. Everyone swam but me, at the Kaanapali Beach Hotel—Island of Maui, and at the Beachboy Hotel Beach–island of Kauai. Carl and I went to Hawaii 1978 and took the children back the last of 1979-80. With the family all together, it was fun. The weather had gotten bad for our first trip. We had to stay overnight in Indianapolis for a flight the next day, and then we had a long lay over in California. Our luggage was on a different flight than ours, which arrived ahead of us. The waiting made the trip more tiring. When our plane landed at Honolulu Airport, we were spirited into a taxi waiting to take us to the Holiday Isle Hotel—what a ride it was!! We were tossed from side to side in the backseat of the taxi; never got to see much. Our arriving late we never received the normal greeting, but were given a Lei each.

The long ordeal was soon forgotten until I got the flu. Carl swam a lot while I pretty much had to stay in our room. The skies and the waters were so blue. It was too nice to have to stay indoors. We did have a balcony that overlooked Honolulu. From the balcony I felt this new breathe of life. The sunsets were so beautiful of varying hues, crimson-pinks mixed with violet-blues. Oh, how peaceful!

My doctor didn't want me to go on my last trip for it was found I needed to have surgery, but I chose to go and be with my family. I am so thankful I made the choice to go and wait for the surgery. We had once made plans to go to China with a group from Purdue University, but my blood pressure was too low to get the shots I needed. It was so disappointing for we had gone through all the preparation to take the trip. This time there was no shots to say I couldn't go.

The children enjoyed the trip and will mention it from time to time. Everything went smoothly; the weather was nice and the flights were on schedule.

The Purdue basketball team was in Hawaii for a basketball tournament. As we always did we went to the game—Purdue won. The people of Hawaii that went to the game cheered for Purdue. When they found out that the children had graduated from Purdue they were so interested. Deb had gotten her Doctorate in Pharmacy, Wil a Biology Degree (premed) and Dan an Associate Degree in Agriculture. Dan didn't want to go to college, but we had told him he had to at least get an associate degree to farm. They each had set a goal early and pretty much stuck with it.

L-R: Wil, Ruby, Deb and Dan "Punchbowl" Pearl Harbor Nat'l Cemetery—Honolulu, Hawaii

Above L-R: Carl, Ruby, Dan, Deb and Wil after feast on Kona Inland at the King Kamehameha Hotel. Christmas & New Years: 1979-1980. Dan & Hawaiian "hula dancer"

Russel and Tillie Miller dressed for "Luau" on Kona

Above: Dan, Carl and Wil. Below: Russel and Dan at the Volcanoes Nat'l Park area

~ CHAPTER 7~

LEARNING TOOLS

*T*here are different tools that are used to aid teaching. Reading is a meaningful gift that changes everything, from a child being able to express themselves to help them go beyond to a journey of self-discovery.

In the first grade Dan was taught the ITA (Initial Teaching Alphabet) way—gilrlz and bois lern to reed with i|t|a. It was a wonderful program that was tried with a group of children. They were taught to spell the way the word sounds. First of all, when a child learns to read, he or she really are learning to break a code—a code in which the letters of the alphabet stand for sounds which makes words they know. For example: Hvv gsv hvmgvmxv rh hslig: means: See the sentence is short. Looks tough—but so does our traditional alphabet to a beginner-reader. The key to the code is that the alphabet is backwards, Z equals A, and so on. The "e" sound is pronounced differently in the words *see, the,* and *sentence,* and is silent at the end of sentence. The "t" sound in "*the*" is not the same sound in *sentence*. A student may be in dismay at having learned the "*A*" in *And* can also look like "*a*". The child is learning at least two alphabets—most capital letters are not shaped like their lower case counter-parts: A-a. If one would take the 26 letters of the English alphabet with caps and lower case and script, you will begin to see the problem some has as a child. The Initial Teaching Alphabet has 44 symbols instead of the conventional 26; each of the 44 symbols represents one and only one sound. The alphabet is basically *phonemic* rather than strictly phonetic. Twenty-four of the 44 symbols are the traditional ones; 14 of the augmentations look very much like two familiar letters joined together. (These are taught to children as individual characters just as we all have been taught to accept w as a separate letter instead of as two v's joined.) The other special symbols represent the remaining phonemes. Our conventional alphabet, 2,000 or more visual patterns are used for the forty-odd sounds of English speech. These 2,000 visual patterns are reduced to only 88 in the ITA. For example, the 22 separate ways of spelling the sound "I," "eye," etc. are represented by only one i|t|a symbol. Therefore, once these 44 symbols are associated with their respective sounds, any word can be read by the child. With this consistent Initial Teaching Alphabet, a child's earlier experience with school demonstrates to him that his reason can be counted on in this basic learning situation—that once he learns a fact, he can apply it successfully. As for the problem of capital letters—which introduce a number of new visual patterns in our traditional system—it doesn't exist.

In i|t|a, a larger version of a letter becomes its capital. Within the design of the letter and its use as a consistent symbol are built other special considerations which reduce the differences between the appearance of words in the Initial Teaching Alphabet and in the conventional alphabet. i|t|a is a special learning tool, not a phonetic alphabet—a tool with built-in devices to make the transition to the spelling children will use for the rest of their lives easy and rapid.

Most children who begin learning to read in the first grade, the transition comes by the end of the first-grade year. A few may make the transfer somewhat sooner. I can proudly say, Dan was reading in the first grade.

Fluency at a third-grade reading level is achieved by a first grader who completes the i|t|a Early–to–Read-Series. When materials written especially for i|t|a students, the Early-to-Read Series, the child in the US transfers by the end of the first year, using i|t|a material which reaches a 4.1 reading level. Children should not be rushed out of i|t|a before they have a chance to reach this fluency level. Traditionally, a reading program introduces a child to only 350 words in his first year of school. An i|t|a child can master 350 words in a few weeks. Dan made an easy transition from i|t|a to the regular alphabet unnoticed and continued on to be an advanced reader. To my knowledge, it was the first time to be taught in Indiana. We were told that it helps children to learn faster. It wasn't continued in the school district after this one teacher quit; it took a special skill to teach i|t|a. The teacher that taught the class was one of the best. When it was introduced to Dan's class, it was the first I had ever heard of it. It was introduced to students in England and later to school districts in the United States.

Wil was reading before he went to school so he had already exceeded the i|t|a obstacle. Normally, spelling is not an important part of the first grade curriculum. Dan got along well and made high grades in spelling. Dan actually wrote in i|t|a—he wrote voluminously! A first grader comes to school able to use thousands of words in conversation. It makes it possible for him or her to read and write any word he can say. In England, i|t|a began in 1960. In September, 1963, classes began in Bethlehem, Pennsylvania. It is a shame it wasn't pursued for it was a good teaching tool. I don't know whether teachers were not interested in pursuing to learn the gift it took to teach it or not. Mrs. Marci Ruwe was a very dedicated teacher that liked challenges. Dan was one of the children from his kindergarten class chosen for the class.

girls and bois lern

tω reed with i|t|a

æ face	b bed	c cat	d dog	ee key
f feet	g leg	h hat	ie fly	j jug	k key
l letter	m man	n nest	œ over	p pen	ɤ girl
r red	s spoon	t tree	ue use	v voice	w window
y yes	z zebra	ʒ daisy	wh when	ch chair
th three	th the	ſh shop	ʒ television	ŋ ring
a father	au ball	a cap	e egg	i milk	o box
u up	ω book	ω spoon	ou out	oi oil

Dan's boredom art work

~ CHAPTER 8 ~

EDUCATION OF LIFE

*W*il and Dan both were placed a grade ahead in their reading. Deb wasn't given a choice the boys had. It was a different school district than she had gone to. It seemed like the school years went so fast. Deb was four years ahead of the boys. She was a freshman at Purdue University by the time the new large school opened. Deb never had a good Chemistry background. Where Deb went to high school there was an Ag teacher that taught chemistry; he had no major in chemistry. The counselors tried to steer students away from Purdue for it was known to be a tough school. The principal worked with Deb and got her into Purdue. With her going into pharmacy without a good chemistry background made it hard. She was real strong in Math and that helped. Deb earned 5 extra credits in Math. Pharmacy was hard, for Deb went through with the veterinarians. She would call home before a test (sometimes crying) saying, "I don't think I'll pass the test."

My response, as I always had said, "Keep those little wheels moving and you will do fine."

Deb was one of nine chosen for the doctorate program at Purdue University. A degree she has put to good use.

While in high school when the secretary, Ellen Faust, had to be gone she would always have Deb to fill in for her. Mrs. Faust, a lovely person, took her secretary job serious.

Deb was named delegate to Girls' State in her junior year. It was quite an honor. Deb got to meet Senator Evan Bayh's late mother, Marvella. Marvella served as President of Girls' Nation. Deb said she was so inspiring and beautiful! Senator Bayh is a two-term Governor of Indiana. Before Evan, his father, Birch Bayh, served as an Indiana senator.

Deb worked in the Pharmacy Library while attending Purdue until rules were changed. It was a job she enjoyed. The children stayed on campus and came home on weekends. We live within a 30 minute driving distance of Purdue University. Weekends meant bags of washing at our house for the boys. Deb did her own at Purdue most of the time. I baked for each so that they would have a snack whenever they were studying. Baking was something that they were use to and I wanted them to have little memories of home.

Dan came home some to help on the farm, but that tapered off. My Pop helped Carl until the mid-afternoon then I would relieve him. There was one year that Deb and I would take turns disking. We'd stop to pick up the rocks, for they are hard on equipment. Carl always has said he liked for Deb or I to disk ahead of the planter for he said it would be smoother when he planted. Perhaps cajoling us with a little flattery persuasion....

I always had a large garden; planting things watching them grow in the spring was always a special time for me. I saw the lawn was taken care of after the boys started to work in the field. There is a lot of work on the farm. I would try to relieve Carl from some of the daily chores. I did all the book work and in the mid-seventies

I started to do our grain contracting. Carl said, "You are better at contracting." That *is* when I *inherited* the job. I still make most of the marketing decisions, but now from time-to-time refer to Dan for I don't care to follow the grain market like I use to. Dan is good at it. I help Dan if he is away from home. The marketing is a crucial part of farming in today's society. There were a few years it was hard to get a grasp on what way to go with a decision and that still applies today. Dan gets a premium for growing waxy corn and seed beans that adds to the income. He is also a sales representative for Pioneer Hi-bred seeds. His father always raised Pioneer seed for he said, "I get a better yield so you don't change what is working for you." Carl is one of the pioneers of its use in our area as well as driving John Deere Equipment.

In June 1988, we encountered a June frost that hit a whole 400 acre area in one field. It was devastating! I had gone to the doctor and upon my return home the sight was just unbelievable. The corn had turned a whitish color. Thank God we had multi-peril insurance based on actual history of production—a good risk coverage.

A bountiful harvest is every farmer's goal. Dan learned as he harvested the soybeans late into the evening, moisture levels went up and yield down. Yields for late-evening harvesting dropped up to 10 bushels per acre due to the beans that were left in the field. Dan noticed the numbers on the yield monitor screen didn't seem as high as they were earlier in the day. He pulled a moisture map and found a trend that hit him like a ton of bricks. The correlation was amazing. Later in the season after the stems dried up more, he didn't see nearly as much difference. To save a glitch that could go undetected, Dan would take the data card home every night to check—not waiting until the end of the season. Yield monitors must be calibrated.

Dan utilized the use of an Earthmaster until recently to attain deep tillage on the soybeans ground in the fall, minimizing with a fewer trips over the field. He plants the soybeans on no-till corn stalks. Dan was taught about values of a sound liming program from his father. Dan uses the variable-rate technology, using GPS and prescription application maps; different than the full broadcast his father had used.

Herbicides have been developed making the many variants of reduced tillage where Dan uses one tillage operation before planting; Earthmaster deep tillage used in place of a moldboard plowing. Dan has changed to no-tillage planting. It will help to minimize unnecessary ground compaction and reduce cost.

The story of agriculture is one of change. It is farmers who make things happen. They are leaving us a good legacy, one based on integrity and fairness. There was a time when farmers were looked at as Hillbillies, Hicks and Clod-hoppers—that doesn't apply today! Most farmers are educated and use their knowledge to the fullest. They continuously study for everything is so Hi-Tech. They'd better know what they are doing, for there is no room for not knowing and to stay in farming in today's society. There has to be a deep desire. Dan's sensibilities, nostalgia and respect for the past makes it peculiarly adept at finding continuities, at making events spring out with new events, new departures take off from our forefather's well-worn path. A view that is not exactly fashionable in today's standards … but it has stood the test of time.

The reason a lot of young people do not recognize an opportunity when they meet it is that they are not ready for the challenge. Dan knew early what he wanted, which helped to get where he is today. There is a lesson to learn of the greatness, beauty, and all wonder of all that is. If a person follows the plan he himself approves and finds interesting, he will then progress more specialty with his life evolutions.

A Spring Time of Flourishing

*Spring time is a season of flourishing greenery, growth
and beauty,*
*A time for the farmer to prepare the seedbed to sow the
seed to bring forth grain—*
*From which He seeks His help to bring forth a rich
yield,*
*So once again, with sweet nostalgia, He can look to
the reborn of a joyous New Spring.*

Ruby M. Gwin

~ Chapter 9 ~

Different Directions
----

*A*dventurous Deborah chose to move out west to Montana where she did hospital work, clinical projects and trained staff project involvements such as patient education, pharmacokinetics and drug information programs. She was instrumental in developing the drug therapy programs in cardiac rehabilitation, dialysis and pulmonary rehabilitation. She traveled and lectured doctors and nurses. Deb is a hands on type person; likes being involved doing something constructive.

Wil and Dan chose to return to Purdue. Wil went on to get a degree in Pharmacy. And Dan said, "I am where I should be," and he got a Bachelor of Science degree in Agriculture Economics; receiving both the associate and his bachelor degrees in three years. Dan always talked-lived farming; it was his dream to one day farm. Deb and Wil always leaned toward medicine.

Wil would later open his own private Pharmacy. Wil just put

the "farm" in pharmacy. Many things applicable in farming are the same as in pharmacy. For an Rx acid soils works for acid stomachs. According to a study showed that an antacid's reaction to stomach acids depends on the type of ion used with the aluminum hydroxide to make the antacid. When carbonate is used, it neutralizes crystalline growth of the aluminum hyroxide, and the antacid stays reactive for a period of months. Other ions, such as sulfate and chloride, lose reactivity much more quickly.

Aluminum hydroxide also can be used to enhance the effectiveness of vaccines. The charge on the aluminum hydroxide ion must be opposite that of the antigen used in the vaccine. This attractive force holds the antigen, allowing the vaccine to effectively produce antibodies. Kidney dialysis patients, who suffer from elevated phosphate levels, also may benefit from the study of aluminum hydroxide. This is just one of many "farm" in pharmacy medical studies that relate to farming. Farming is the backbone of the country.

Wil's wife, Melissa, and I helped out at the new pharmacy. Melissa was also working at her nursing job at the time. She is very talented in whatever she does. She is quite gifted with her hands—in liken to her father, an orthopedic surgeon. Her mother died when she was nine. She says her Grandma Gutwein became her foundation. Melissa decided to advance further her nursing career and will soon have a Nurse Practitioner's degree.

Wil and Deb have worked together for over 11 years. They do a lot of compounding for both doctors and veterinarians. I am proud of our children, for each are very caring individuals. I tried to teach each what I had been taught; if anything was worth doing, it was worth doing right. Do what makes you happy and do your best. These words would color my being a mother. I made mistakes along the way—but I learned!

The family always had a good time at meal time. Carl liked his ice cream, pie, cake and cookies. We never had lunch or dinner without a dessert. The children told Carl if he wanted ice cream he'd have to run around the house. He would bundle up in freezing cold weather and run around the house. They had a lot of fun teasing their father about his dessert—he enjoyed every minute of it! I have always baked a lot ... much to their delight.

One day, when Dan was quite small; Carl had left early to do some work for his father. It was a little later that the phone rang. It was our neighbor wanting to know if Dan was home.

I responded that he was in bed. Bernice said, "Are you sure?"

I replied, "Yes, but I will go check." She said she could see a small child with a red hood moving fast along the side of the road. I went to check his room and he wasn't there. I knew it was Dan, for he had a red hooded sweatshirt. He had gotten up, dressed himself, and slipped out of the house. I immediately returned to the phone to tell her I'd be right there.

Meanwhile, Bernice watched the direction Dan was headed—*I knew*! I pick her up and she told me his where-a-bouts at that time. When he would see a car coming he'd get down in the ditch to hide. He had gone north and turned east. Bernice said he was sure moving at a fast pace.

Boy! He wasn't a very happy boy when he saw me! He was really upset that his father went to grandpas without him. It was hard to get him in the car. I had had surgery and was unable to handle him in which made it hard for Bernice, for he was determined he was going to where his father was and tried to get away. She finally got him in the car! What a savior my neighbor was deviating Dan's risky mission!

Dan had gotten close to a state highway that he would have had to cross. I do believe he would have gotten to grandpas. Yet to this day, it is a puzzle how he got up, dressed himself and slipped out of the house without me knowing. Thank God he dressed warm, for it was cold out. He always thought when the equipment left the house he should get to go. Of course, Grandpa Gwin thought it was funny—I didn't! It was quite scary, but he never did it again. I was one to always keep a check on the children. He says he just about got caught and he got back under the covers and waited with his clothes on. He escaped around the house when I went to the mailbox to mail out some letters. Children can move like lighting when they are on a mission. He will still say, "He, Dad, wasn't supposed to go without me [*laughs*]!"

Dan's first farm experience was disking on the farm where he now lives. He was riding with Carl on the tractor and kept at his father to let him disk. Carl stopped the tractor and went over and hooked up the 3020 tractor to a disk and put Dan on the tractor for the first time by himself. Dan was having trouble with the corners, so Carl stopped his tractor and went over to Dan and asks, "What are those pedals?"

Dan responded, "Brakes!"

Carl said, "Use them!"

Dan still remembers what his father told him; from that moment, Dan was on his own. I know the first time I drove the tractor was cultivating. After my first initial tractor gear lesson, I was turned lose to the hard job of cultivating—learning on my own not to cultivate out the corn or soybean rows. Carl certainly knew how to teach a person, cultivating of all things! It would never become a favorite job … I just did it and never complained.

There were times Dan would say he didn't feel like going to school, but later in the morning he would feel like driving the tractor. This didn't happen a lot—just now and then. Dan made good grades. He never had to work hard to get them. There were times Dan did have migraines. I finally noticed the days he ate a hot dog at school, he would get a migraine. He stopped eating them, and we noticed the days missed were very few. We had started to believe that he was playing hooky to drive the tractors. He still wanted to be there when the tractors went to the field, but we learned he did have a valid reason for staying home.

I have a lot of art work Dan did while he was in elementary and junior high. He would draw pictures of football players, TV stars, comic cartoons characters, trucks and cars. I call them his school "boredom" artwork. He sure used a lot of paper as I did. I was always drawing in school or at home.

There are many good memories when the children were little. I remember at our church one Sunday there was a visiting black minister. Willie was around 5 years old. Willie was always a quizzical child. He asked the minister his name and the minister replied, "Puddin' Tame ask me again and I'll tell the same."

Of course, the minister was teasing with Wil. Wil ask again, and the minister responded smilingly with the same answer. Wil just looked up at the minister with a quizzical look not to ask again. The minister never did tell him his name. I expected Wil to say something, but he never did.

When Wil was twelve or thirteen he wrote a song with both the words and notes. I never knew he wrote it until I found it. The title is "God's Magnificent Work". I decided it warranted a copyright. I look at it sometimes just for a lift. It makes me feel with such pride to know at his young age he had chosen such beautiful choice of words to write. Sometimes, parents don't always know their children's thinking. They never cease to amaze you. Deb played the piano and Wil played the guitar for the school quartet. Wil was a seven-eighth grader and Deb was a junior-senior.

Deb, while attending Purdue along with Gene L. O'Hara, Pharm D., got an article published that they co-wrote. For an undergraduate it's quite an honor to get something published, yet—it can be a no-no! Deb was recruited several times to teach at Purdue. They visited our home to talk with her, but she didn't want to teach. In her last year she taught students in pharmacy classes. Students said she was not only patient but she was good at conveying to them. Deb is a patient person as well as compassionate—sympathetic to others distress. She is not a judgmental type person. She would have been a good teacher, but it wasn't what she wanted or planned to do when she chose the School of Pharmacy.

Each day when the children came in the house after they got off the school bus they would call out, "Mom". I would answer and that was all they wanted to know—*Mom was home.*

There was this one particular day that Wil and Dan came home wanting their savings. Puzzled by it, I asked, "Why?"

They explained that at school the children were making fun of a boy and it bothered them both. The boy's teeth protruded out so bad that it was hard for the boy to speak. This touched my heart, our sons caring and thinking of another. I talked it over with Carl, and we both felt if it meant that much to the boys to ask and want to use their savings that we would have something done—providing it was okay with both the boy and his parents. I called the school and made the arrangements to have everything taken care of and ask that our name not be revealed. We were shown the progress of the work as it was being done. It really helped the boy in his future years for it gave him a chance to have a decent job. After he was married his wife made it a mission to find out who did the deed for her husband. I was thanked once when I was in the store many years later. I told him it was Wil and Dan that wanted it done; that I was happy it worked out for him. He is still working at the business place where he saw me.

The boy's father had a very bad heart condition. There was no way the family could have paid to have the correction done for it also called for surgery. It was a happy meeting—I never knew him or that he worked there. One day, when I was working at the pharmacy the orthodontist, Dr. Garry Hamilton who helped with the dental work came in and told me what we did saved the boy's life. That was what we wanted, for the young boy had been through some rough years.

The children and I would pick up ear corn after the combine and would take it to the elevator. One year when a big high line went through, they knocked down a path of corn several feet wide. Of course, that was easy gathering with plenty of easy corn to pickup. Back then, the elevators would buy the ear corn. We didn't have livestock to turn out into the fields to utilize the down corn. The children would save their money by starting a bank savings account. It was that savings the boys were asking for.

We learned from that experience; giving to help others gives one a sense of peace. We now give or do something each year for someone. I was raised believing in giving and doing for others.

When Dan got to come home for a weekend from the hospital, he would bring another boy from the Methodist Hospital that had been injured. The other boy had a higher up injury than Dan. He had been in an automobile accident and had received a seat belt injury. He was considered a low-level quad. He had just a small incision about 2 inches long at the lower neck. Dan has lost all contact with David. David was younger than Dan. He was from a divorced family. His father and stepmother were the ones that seem to look out for him. I remember him saying he was trying to learn to bake a cake with a box mix. Patients were taught to be as independent as possible. It would have been a hard job for David to bake for he didn't have good use of his hands.

Some of the injured on the Spinal Cord Unit had dysfunctional families. There was a fellow that had not had an injury, but was paralyzed after having surgery. He was probably in his late fifties. One day I found him crying; he said his wife didn't want him home. He and Dan became friends. We don't know if he got better or not for his family didn't really want contact.

There was a young black boy, Terry Washington that had been shot in a random shooting. The only time the family came was to get him to sign a check. It was so sad to see innocent victims have to endure the life they would have to live. When Terry would push his call button for help it would go unanswered. Dan got where he would push his button and tell them Terry needed help. This is one thing Dan will talk about. These things seemed to be permeated in Dan's mind leaving much compassion that many would not understand.

There was a nurse that had been shot by her estranged husband. She was leaving the hospital where she worked when he shot her and then killed himself. It was a high-up injury where she had to use an electric chair. She tried to help others as she was used of doing—duty call! She had two young teenage daughters. I have wondered many times about how she continued to cope. Her sister from out of state was going to take her back home with her. She was a very pretty lady.

We have someone dear to our heart that was found lying in some grass underneath a bridge over a popular biking and hiking trail. She is a ranking federal public defender for the U.S. District Court in the state where she lives. They have ruled out a possible spinal injury as well as brain damage, but she has a long road to go. She will have to have cosmetic surgery. When found by two walkers they couldn't tell if it was a young man or women and called 911. She had been severely beaten—an act of violence that is so infuriating!

A very pretty, petite and talented person; it really hurts to know she was attacked in such a brutal way. In her chosen field she handled high-profile cases. She has been taught with a strong work ethic. With her training, I know she will stay focused continuing to galvanize and energize others as she did before. I pray they get the responsible person.

Her parents are retired professional people. I feel for them, for I can understand in part what they have and are going through. I know they want the person caught, but their main concern is for their daughter. I know they were very distressed at this time. You want to take away the pain, but one just has to ask for the courage to be brave for your loved one's sake. It is truly hard to be near unable to do something, but that is when you have stay true to your faith.

It used to be safe to ride a bike or walk where a person would want to go. As a child, we never did lock our doors because we knew who our neighbors were. Imagine doing that today even in a small town—not in today's society! This type of offense seems to be more prevalent today. It hurt when Dan was injured, but it didn't happen through malice. He was getting ready to do something constructive when his accident happened. It is always so hard to see something that has happen so unnecessary and how it affects everyone concerned. There is so much vindictiveness and malice in the world. Every time you look at a newspaper or turn on the TV or radio you hear where someone committed a crime against someone. Crimes that are intended to cause anguish or hurt—with no remorse! Our society has changed, to avoid the shades of grey I hold fast to the belief of good.

I had a bad experience as a child that was most unheard of. I was visiting at another family's home when I was grabbed by a young man. It was in the late morning hours and I was outside when it happened. God only knows how I got away—for I was around nine. There was a lot of searching the area. Even my brother went searching down the road on his bicycle with the okay from State Trooper, Sgt. Bob Alenduff. I remember there was a lot of questioning which made it all worse to have to relive it day after day. Finally the day came when Sgt. Alenduff, a family friend, returned and told mother it had been an escaped German prisoner from Hoopeston, Illinois about 20 miles west.

During World War II many of the captured German soldiers were processed to the United States. Some were placed in Hoopeston, Illinois at the canning factory.

For me, there was no closure, for I was too young. I was frightened, my left arm hurt for a long time. My mother spent many nights at my bedside, for I exhibited withdrawal. Her loving touch helped quiet the mind and shelter the fear. Carl told me recently that I am not over what happened in my earlier years. That surprised me, for I never talked about it. I have rough nights. There wasn't counseling back then as there is today.

I find the study of scientific knowledge to legal problems interesting. It has always been an interest of mine. Profiling study I think would be so rewarding; just to be able to relate to or dealing with solving a crime, to find a solution, explanation or finding an answer. I like author Patricia Cornwell and enjoy watching Dayle Hinmam, FBI trained crime profiler's work. Cornwell helped establish the Virginia Institute of Forensic Science and Medicine; first forensic training facility of its kind in the nation. Cornwell is a ward-winning crime reporter and worked as a computer analyst in the chief medical examiner's office in Virginia.

I have meet an interesting fella named, Dennis Weaver, which I truly admire. He has quiet a résumé. He served in the U.S. Army and 23 years as a Special Agent with the FBI. Dennis now helps John Walsh find missing children in the National Center for Missing & Exploited Children. He told me he watches very closely when it comes to dealing with children … a special gift I know that he has. Perhaps it is his work, but I feel a special closeness to Dennis. Dennis, wife Shelia, and Shelia's parents have become our good friends. Carl knew Shelia's father from World War II.

~ CHAPTER 10 ~

A PREDETERMINED COURSE

*S*pinal cord injures occur from malice; sports; falls; knife and gunshot wounds; automobile, motorcycle, and farm accidents; and explosions—life changed forever. A paralytic cannot feel and is unable to tell if they have been injured. Dan gets leg spasms, an uncontrollable contraction of one spasm or more in the muscles. Spasms can be caused by infections, fatigue or tension. Spastic paralysis, a weakness of a limb or limbs associated with increased reflex activity. The brain also reacts to any kind of stimulation. Dan will move about every 15 minutes to prevent what we call pressure sores or decubitus ulcers. Vigilant care is necessary at all time. Sustaining pressure on parts of the body cuts off circulation, within hours damaging tissue is dead. A paraplegic may not know anything is wrong for pressure sores may not be visible for a few days or weeks. Dan watches what type of cushion he sits on and checks for any redness that may develop. He gives it a concerted effort by maintaining a good care program and uses the resources of what may be beneficial to him.

These days what mystifies me are the many human tragedies that are at times within one's own control. Technological advances and their substitution don't change it. They are cheating themselves and really there isn't much anyone can do about it.

There were some people, farmers and family that visited or called Dan just to know his condition to never come or contact him again. Dan finds many will shy away from him—he feels they don't know what to say. There is a couple, Laura and Kevin Gross that invited Dan into their home and would take him different places after his injury. They even constructed a wheelchair ramp for Dan's use. It is so refreshing to find those like Ty Nannet who still has the time to be kind. Friendship is so priceless—a gift that can't be bought or sold. Ty went to see Dan at the hospital all the while he was in the hospital—reaching out a hand when Dan needed it. Ty and his wife's family use to own a local hardware.

A niece, Lora Ellen, and husband, Tim Budd, were there with much support. Tim really helped with whatever he could. He was there when help was needed. Dan's Uncle, Bill Gwin, had written to say he would be coming to see Dan when they returned from Florida. He and his wife, Mary, always spent their winters in Florida. Bill had a heart attack and passed away. He never got to see Dan. Bill had a heart condition but it was an unexpected loss. He would call to check on Dan and see if there was any progress change. A faithful heart loves, speaks and helps by thinking of others ... medicine of life.

There is a certain physical world Dan no longer has; each day is a challenge with no competing. Challenges are how we learn and progress. Everyday is not necessarily good. At times I still am overwhelmed at Dan's ability to treat each day as a new day. A spinal cord injury with lasting effects will cause drastic change in one's life. Vocational rehabilitation programs provide guidance and training. There is a spiritual healing emotionally. While Dan was in the hospital he had been set up to have counseling and guidance, but Dan refused. The psychiatrist said he wasn't accepting his disability. Dan proved not just to himself but everyone that he was and could deal with his injury. Some would and did require the need for counseling in dealing with their injury. I do believe it would have hindered more than helped Dan, for he had chosen to look forward working toward returning home. Dan never developed conversion disorder disability from his injury, but started working on a goal plan treatment. Occupational therapy depends on motivation … Dan was ready for whatever was thrown at him. In therapy there were many different types of disabilities: people trying to sit, people learning to roll over, breathing exercises, amputees learning to walk using their prostheses. Dan also had to learn going up steps.

For me, I don't know how he could do what he did, or how he did it. Dan may have had a feeling of helplessness, but he never was in denial of his injury. Being inactive there is a significant loss of bone density. The bowel program each day takes an hour, plus, he has to deal with catheter change or the use of one. Dan drinks a lot of fluids, which is essential to keep the kidneys healthy. Dan takes large dosages of vitamin C. It has helped him to ward off bladder infections. Dan is very consciously aware of his care and stays focused with self-discipline.

After Dan came home he experienced a lot of bladder infections until he went to our family doctor, Dr. Leak. He gave Dan some pointers and suggested he take vitamin C. When Dan went back to the specialist for a checkup, he asks Dan what he was doing different and Dan told him. The specialist said, "That's good that it works for you."

Dan still has infections, but nothing like they were after he returned home from the hospital. He takes cranberry tablets that are also good for the prevention of bladder infections. Dr. Leak was really concerned with Dan's many infections and he said, "If they continued he could end up on dialysis." It was a blessing to see them taper off. Dr. Leak is not only a gifted doctor, but a person with many talents. It would have been good to have had him on the case immediately after Dan's injury. He said, "The first thing I would have done was get the swelling down." He was a doctor that thought beyond a situation.

Dan is grateful for the care that he got at the Methodist Hospital. Dr. Feuer was there with him each step of the way even after his return home. It was a special doctor and patient relationship that shall always be remembered.

The Methodist Hospital wasn't like being home, but Dan was where he needed to be. He worked hard to get where he was so soon. The time for him probably seemed like an eternity. He has had to learn "patient faith." There are some business places that he has to set and wait for service in his pickup do to accessibility. He never complains. Dan understands a business place can't stop what they are doing to just care for his needs because of his handicap situation, nor does he expect them to.

Dan has reframed his entire concept of attending to business; he has learned new ways to planning ahead making decisions. This enables him to get things done in a more orderly manner. Dan's injury became more a source of leadership inclinations. He has had to reach out as never before. He has recognized that he can't do the things that he once did and has learned to work around his weaker areas. The basis for his success: Dan started by believing in his ability. He learned to seize opportunities with family support to cheer him forward. It called for mental toughness. Dan wasn't afraid to take chances—obstacles he learned to handled along the way by being realistic. He focused on what he could control—he defiantly is a risk taker in some areas! There seems to be no doubts or fears; he took a predetermined course. If there were doubts or "dark fears" Dan never expressed or showed it.

Through Dan's pain and sorrow, Carl's and my faith were tested along with Dan's. Each of us at sometime will walk through "darkness." It took strength to face what lay ahead for Dan, but like the seed Dan had sown to bring forth grain, we must do the same thing. Life does have its suffering and pain—part and parcel of life! Making everyday count for something; NEW HOPE is born within when one who has the courage, faith and the strength when in the hours of darkness to valiantly keep on trying. Not everyone has that source of strength to look ahead beyond....

I think it was good for Dan to get home and be around familiar surroundings. Once at home there wasn't much idle time. It wasn't long before he was called upon and responded whenever a call came from rehab where there was a patient that needed a pep talk. This makes me proud, for as I stated, he had been told he wasn't accepting his injury. I feel with this special caring for others, it helped Dan in his own battle. He challenges himself and goes for, one would think, the impossible. Some things are difficult for Dan, but he recognizes them and focuses on what he can do to change them. It is the command of direction which Dan took that was energizing for everyone. He saw it as his only chance, the sole way by which he could gain the amount of positive knowledge which was indispensable for his own purpose. It was as if—why let efforts go to waste?

His pushing a positive practice was comfort for Carl and me. Having patience was mitigated by the satisfaction of seeing progress he could make by planning. Slowly but surely throughout his ordeal he took instant action on looking ahead, full of spirited energy, impassioned with the desire to gain occupational freedom as much as he could.

One of Dan's best known stories in that of his leadership prescience of what he was going to do. He never once demanded for attention. It was more like he took the initiative looking and seeking to bring forth a rich harvest on *the wings to succeed*. One can not cease to admire him for his burning determination after his near death experience. He has never asked *why*, only says *there was a purpose*. He has never dwelled on his injury. The very life—that almost-life can go on is how Dan is living—one grateful day at a time.

Dr. Feuer talked with and told Dan how things were. He was straight forward with Dan. I think for Dan this was important for Dr. Feuer had said, "Dan is smart; he realizes his condition." Dan has never spoken about what happened on that cold, icy day eighteen years ago to his father or me. He started working in a positive way where he could move on to higher ground telling his father what needed to be taken care of.

I think Doctor Feuer was a good mentor for Dan in the way he challenged Dan early on. All patients aren't as lucky as Dan to have a doctor of such caliber as Dr. Feuer—one that gives 100%. I think each working together found the challenge an "exhilarating" gift of HOPE!

In whatever arena of life one may meet, each has to believe in the power to lead, to inspire, and to bring about success. Dan had to decide himself the course he would take. Dan certainly showed us all grace under affliction. There was no wallowing around in self-pity, but looked for solutions, and moved on learning to be mentally tough.

After those first few weeks I felt like the luckiest mother in the world to see Dan take the high road, for it had been as though I were on a slow moving train to no where. You can't walk through the valley without growing spiritually—which helped Dan to guide the course.

Dr. Henry Feuer, a Neurosurgeon that attended to Dan after his transfer to the Methodist Hospital in Indianapolis, Indiana. He became Dan's rock.

~ CHAPTER 11 ~

A SPECIAL COURSE

We were a family that worked together and enjoyed what we did. It seemed like we always had a project going. Families that do things together have a special bond. I feel that helped Dan chose a path of brightness and challenge that helped not only himself, but his family to deal with his injury. He embraced the challenge and looked at it as an opportunity, not a setback. Dan's decision was one for criticism, but he stayed true to his belief and vision and decided to lead accordingly. He did understand some of the people's thoughts, for they had never been where he was at to make decisions as he had to do. It makes a difference! It was either give in to not trying or to try.

Although, very capable, Dan didn't want to be desk bound. He had always been an active person doing physical work. If he had, too, he would have, but not without proving to himself first he could *no* longer farm. Dan, a determined person, always knew what his calling was—to farm! Goals are only made through determination.

Dan always has new projects in the making or doing. He fixed a platform to put on the forklift so he can be lifted up to paint equipment. He is very artistic and a perfectionist.

Carl was getting Dan out of the sprayer (by moving his legs) one day, when Dan said, "It has been sixteen years since my legs would do what I wanted them to do." It wasn't a regret remark–just a matter of fact. A rare statement! It was the first time Dan had ever mentioned about not being able to use his legs after what he said to his father while waiting for the ambulance. Dan learned soon sometimes one has to apply teaching to one's life.

We have never heard Dan say there's no purpose now. Whereas one may think, there is not much life to look toward, but for Dan he just chose to look for new channels and meet each directly on. He never asks anyone to do small things for him without trying himself. He tries to make himself as independent as one can.

I was very concerned when Dan would move alongside of his pickup bed and load his wheelchair. He would use his leg braces that come up thigh high on his legs. Then he'd have to use his upper body to swing himself to move his legs, for he cannot balance himself unless he is holding onto something. He is pretty independent with wanting to do things himself. Last year he got another pickup. It has an extended cab that he now puts his wheelchair in. It has leather seats that are an advantage for Dan when he gets in and out off the seat.

Dozer spray painted by Dan in 2005.

~ CHAPTER 12 ~

SPECIAL BOND

*I*t was through Dan's friendship with Gary Standiford he met and married the spirited, Georgia girl, Donya Lester in 1995. Donya is the Executive Secretary of Purdue University Ag Alumni Association. Gary Standiford is the District Director for the Purdue Alumni Board of Directors. Dan had heard Donya speak at a few events. He admired her ability, for she is a wonderful speaker. I am not sure how their meeting came about, but she would come out and ride the combine while Dan was picking corn. She said, "When I looked up and saw those blue eyes and that smile—he stole my heart."

It takes a lot of adjustment in a situation as Dan and Donya's. They both have a sense of humor. They are a lot of fun—both pretty entertaining! She got her degree in Animal Science from the University of Georgia and a master's degree in animal breeding and genetics from Virginia Tech University. I was at the Mayo Clinic in Minnesota when Donya and Dan met.

In 2001 Dan and Donya asked Carl and me to go to the Outback Bowl with them in Florida—we sure had a lot of fun. Our grandson, Tom, also went with us. Before Tom was to return home, Dan and Donya thought it would be fun to get Tom a fake earring. When Tom got off the airplane the earring did fool his parents at first. Tom said, "I didn't let the joke go *too* far!" Dan and Donya have a habitual fondness for joking with just good humor!

I had never seen much of Florida. It was raining when Carl and I were there years ago. Donya and Dan rented a car to drive. Donya drove us around taking us to the Fort Myers area. We visited the Edison-Ford Winter Estates—Donya said, "Now I know what Mom likes." It was so enjoyable; I do like (love) history! She drove us around this beautiful Sanibel Island area; one of her favorite places! I got to wondering if Dan and I would have to come home alone, for Carl really liked the island too. The scenery was very pretty. The water was so blue, like the sky! As we headed back to Tampa-St. Petersburg area, we found a nice fish place where we ate. It was so relaxing and the food was good.

In the Tampa area, we all went out to eat the night before Tom's departure the next day. We all ordered a steak dinner that Carl and I say was the best steak we have ever eaten in a restaurant. Tom had a flight schedule two days ahead of our leaving. He and I sure had a fun time at the Purdue Ag Alumni dinner. The whole trip was a memorable one—thanks to our children. The next year we went with them to California to the Rose Bowl. We didn't have the fun that we had in Florida. The Rose Bowl Parade wasn't as enjoyable as we thought it would be. We did enjoy being together.

Donya and Dan's wedding picture—1995

As the Executive Secretary of Purdue University Ag Alumni Association, many nights you will find Donya driving down a lonesome, dark stretch of highway with the foot somewhat heavy in her job of speaking to various different organizations with various topics: Purdue Agriculture, life as a farmer's wife, agriculture volunteering or a Farm Bureau group. Her topic depends on her audience.

Top L-R: Donya, Dan, Carl and Tom at "Outback Bowl". Bottom: Donya, Dan and a Purdue fan standing along side of Purdue's "Boilermaker Special"—2001.

Dan has never let his disability hinder any of his travel. He is able to travel. He does have to watch for hotel accessibility. He and Donya have been overseas. He tries to live as normal life as possible. When they travel and rent a car Donya has to drive, for Dan has to have hand controls installed to operate a vehicle.

Dan went once to Las Vegas and San Francisco to see a brotherly friend that went to Purdue. Purdue is where Dan and Wil met Dino Bordigioni and Pete Quinn. Dino was a football player until he had a head injury and quit. He was in Wil's wedding. After Dino graduated from Purdue, he returned home to Las Vegas before moving to San Francisco, where he had a Harley-Davidson business.

Dino took Dan around San Francisco in one of his unusual sidecars. Everyone to the Japanese tourist would stop to look and take pictures. They went down this unique (Lombard) street that zig-zag around-and-around where most of the streets were up-and-down. Dino went across the Golden Gate Bridge (designed by a Purdue University engineer) that is a strait 2 miles leading into San Francisco Bay from the Pacific Ocean. They went down this street called Ashbury-Haight. It is commonly called "The Haight" or "The Shopping District". In the '60s era, it was the epicenter of the *hippy* culture. The area is subdivided into the *Upper Haight* and the *Haight-Fillmore* or *Lower Haight* districts. San Francisco has beautiful residential homeowners' districts. Dan really enjoyed the trip and said, "Oh, shucks, we had fun!"

The trip was not only good, but the right timing. It was after his injury, and it was his first experience traveling by air.

After Dan's injury, Dino brought Pete Quinn to visit Dan. We sure enjoyed their visit. They ate lunch with us ... football players can eat! I prepared well for the day. It was a fun day. Pete was a good football player at Purdue and now a radio sports announcer for the Purdue football games. During the fall harvesting, Dan faithfully tunes in and listens to Pete while combining.

Dino sold his business and has traveled to different parts of the country on his motorcycle. The last time he talked with Dan he said he was going to start writing. Knowing Dino his book will be interesting!

Dino use to come every year but has been busy enjoying life surroundings. He called one day to talk to Dan and Carl happened to answer the phone. Dino told Carl he just got back from riding his Harley-Davidson to the southern tip of South America. He said he had been away a year and was surprised to see how different here at home was. Dino tries to come each year for Purdue's Football "Homecoming" game in October. That is when we see him. He is always a happy face to see; as we are his "Hoosier" parents!

One night, while Dan and Wil were at Purdue, Wil and a football player, Bill Kay, came out to the farm. Bill having run his car through water puddles caused the muffler to clog up. The car didn't have enough power so Bill had to push the car up 4th Street hill in Lafayette, Indiana, while Wil drove. Bill was a strong boy! He wasn't tired when he got to our house—he was having fun! They had to disconnect the muffler before returning to Purdue.

Bill was a tall, good looking boy, from the ghetto district in Maywood, Chicago, Illinois area. After graduating from Purdue Bill went on to play pro-football in Texas. Bill continued to play pro for a few years. We have lost contact of his whereabouts. As for Dino, he is a person that enjoys life to the fullest!

Dan ate a lot of pizza while at Purdue. There were many nights Dan would order Domino's pizza that he shared with Dino or some of the other boys. Wil and Dan roomed together, but Wil was never around much for he worked on different projects. Dan still remembers Domino's telephone number. It is interesting how some things we never forget!

Wil teases Deb that Dan and he would call her about every night so she wouldn't have a reason to call to check up on them! She is razzed by Wil—plenty at work. Deb is 4½ years older than Wil and he will tell her—that makes her over the hill! He tells everyone that she is his *much older* sister. Dan, too, still does his share of teasing her when he gets a chance. In fact, it's the first thing he does when he sees her—she just says something back and laughs.

The children always enjoyed teasing the other. One day, while living on campus Wil had taken the Cordoba that the boys had on campus to a high rise residence hall. Dan and another boy happened to see the car. Dan decides to pull a trick on Wil. Using his keys, he jumps in the car, and drove it to the end of the street and around the corner. The two watched for Wil to come out of the residence hall to see his reaction.

Dan says, "It was worth a million bucks to watch Wil when he came out. Wil was getting frantic, so I hollered telling him where the car was before he'd decide to call the police." I am not sure whether Wil was ticked or laughed about what Dan had done—I bet Wil got even! They roomed together through their time spent at Purdue.

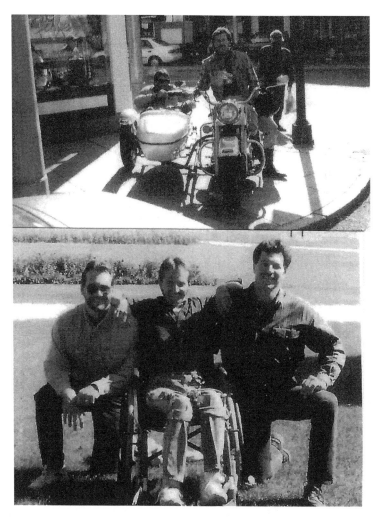

Above: Dino on his Harley-Davidson riding Dan around San Francisco in the cycle's sidecar. Below: Pete Quinn, Dan and Dino Bordigioi.

Above: Dan sitting in the sidecar along the San Francisco Bay. Below: Golden Gate Bridge in San Francisco

~ CHAPTER 13 ~

CARING IN A SPECIAL WAY

$\mathcal{D}$an, before he and Donya were married, gave money to a social service worker in our county for gifts for the needy children at Christmas. Dan and Donya don't have any children. At Christmas time, they have spent hours shopping for the children at Cary Home in Lafayette, Indiana. Some children don't ask for anything but little things "such" as socks. Dan and Donya would get what the children wanted and then they would add a real nice gift that they had not asked for. Each child would have a few gifts to open up.

At Donya's work they learned what she and Dan were doing and wanted to help, so Donya came up with an idea for a cook book. She collected recipes from the Agricultural Department employees and typed up the recipes for a local printer to print up. He donated the printing of the books. They were a nice book—well put together.

What a gift—making a child that doesn't have, happy! There are so many children out there could and would love to have a home. I think it is good for children to learn to buy a gift at Christmas for a needy child. Our grandchildren have been taught the gift of giving. Deb and Wil's children are taught to buy a gift with their *own* money. Wil's children give to "Operation Christmas Child" and Deb's son gives a gift to a needy child at church. It not only teaches them to care, but they learn how rewarding it is to share with someone that doesn't have. There are a lot of children here in the United States that are going without. We always hear about how other countries need, but not here at home. If one would just visit the children's ward in a hospital or children's home, it would break your heart. It is absolutely devastating.

One day, our trustee came to the place where I worked and ask if I would take in a (court awarded) child that was being removed from a home with five children. There were three boys and two girls. I never had to think about it for there was no way that I could have said *no* when a child was in need of a home. Unexpectedly, the welfare brought Tommy to the business place while I was working. I had to leave and take him home for he was dirty. In my bathing him, I found he had a large cut on his stomach that the welfare never had attended to. Tommy had been in their care for four days. The cut was all red and infected, and he had to be taken to the doctor. Tommy had tried to hide under the bed to keep the social workers from taking him is how he got the cut. It certainly was a terrifying time for little Tommy with so much adjustment.

These little children were good children. Deb was only two and Tommy was four. I had him over three years. I shall never forget when he left, for he had become my child. I took it hard. Carl took me to visit him, but quit; it was hard for Tommy and I. Tommy would run away after seeing me. I tried to take Tommy's memory and find the courage to be strong with knowing I gave my best to him while he was in my care. It was some years later that Tom located me. One evening I just so happen to answer the phone and the voice on the other end said, "Mom, this is Tom." I knew instantly who it was.

Today, Tommy is a mixed up adult; a child, one of many lost in the system. I am a person that feels thoughtfulness is a virtue and the joy of giving is its reward. I can only thank the trustee, for giving me that short period in Tommy's life. I just wish Tommy's life could have been different. I still remember the joy on his face when I would fix lemon pie. I quit making it for it was too much of a memory of that smiling, little face with a gleam in those dark brown eyes when he saw I had made him lemon pie. Our son, Wilson, named his only son Thomas (Tom) Carl. I know it was for my benefit. Although quite young; Wil was old enough to remember our going to see Tommy. The time Tommy spent in our lives was a growing one.

I've learned that not only are there many children in need, but also adults. I have been going to the nursing home to see my brother and I try to take time to visit with some of the others there. Some don't have anyone that comes to see them. There was one fellow that had two sons that never did come to see him during the three years he was at St. Mary Healthcare Center. This is so hard for me to fathom; they both lived there in town. He was a kind man. Melissa went to visit him with me, for Ernie knew her Grandpa Gutwein and her father when he was in med-school. The visit meant a lot to them both. Melissa asked Ernie if he had known her mother—unfortunately he hadn't.

This all makes me think back to the different reactions when Dan was injured. I would like for us to become a more caring, compassionate nation. Showing that you care is the best gift one can give!

I met a young fellow, Christopher "Chris" Kennedy at the nursing home while visiting my brother. At the time I was unaware that I knew his father, Pat. When going to school, we lived only about two miles apart from each other. Chris had a liver ailment. He was so sweet; he made you want to take a hold of him and keep hugging him.

There were two St. Mary's therapists that accompanied Chris to the Purdue-Ball State basketball game played at Purdue University. What a thoughtful act of kindness! There were cheerleaders and band members that came up to the handicap area to visit with Chris. Christopher participated in Special Olympics, and was on a three-time state champion basketball team. It was a nice day for Chris. Chris's father, Pat, graduated from Purdue.

Chris (my buddy) will be truly missed, for Chris lost his hard fought battle. I feel so blessed for our last visit together. Christopher could hardly speak above a whisper; I had to lean down close to understand him for he was so weak. I started to leave for I wanted him to keep his strength, but he didn't want me to go. He asks me to wait a few minutes. I just stood there brushing his short, dark, black hair back, then a nursing assistant name, Donna Hicks and another came in to get him up. I leaned down kissed his forehead and told him I loved him. I admired him so much. He shall always be remembered by all of us whose life he so dearly touched—our lives *all* have been enriched!

There is a certified nursing assistant, Cindy Henry that helped my brother, Harold, with his adjustment at first. He would go out at night and talk with the nurses and as well as Cindy. They have become his family. He says everyone is nice. One caring person, as Cindy, whether it is an adult or a young person can make all the difference in the world, opening up opportunities that may have seemed unreachable. The way we treat people is the way we get treated in return. Just something like a gentle hand touch or a kind word means so much to those that are in need.

A roommate of Harold's passed away recently. His wife, Maxine Webster was from our area. Our daughter and she went golfing recently. We never knew her husband had passed away until Maxine called Deb. I told Deb that Maxine liked to golf so when Deb was visiting her uncle the two met and talked. Deb said she enjoyed their outing. It had been sometime since Deb had played golf. She had talk about going but she never got around to going. Our daughter's reaching out in a connecting way offered a communication of inspiration; an act that would end being inspiring for both she and Maxine.

I am a mother that liked to talk, listen and just visit with the children. All three would talk with me. I am the huggy type. We never get off the phone without saying—I love you! Our four grandchildren are the same way.

Living and learning go hand–in-hand today emphasizing a family sharing a strong base to teach and lead with love. Love speaks louder than words. A parent's love emphasizes quality, not equality. My one pet peeve is parents favoring one child. I am a mother that is on all their sides. Families should be a team—learning to build and doing things together. Mothers and fathers have a way sometimes preaching ethics and morals, but I felt it starts at home. It is important for parents to watch and catch the right moment to emphasize values and honesty. It isn't always easy for parents to choose between what's right and what's wrong. Children need to learn relationship is never one way. What is done to children, they will do to society. We mothers are a testing ground for our children. As the saying goes—a mother's work is never done! It's kind of like you take "One Day at a Time".

Today those words apply to *many* fathers that have the responsibility with household chores and caring for the children. Many men in today's society are the stay at home *mom*. They do the cooking, caring for the children and the household chores while the women are earning the income or they have won custody of their children. The best gift a parent can give a child is to let them know *someone cares.*

Today, families don't spend quality time together like when I was growing up, or when our children were home. Dinner (supper) hour at our house was a time I always looked forward to. I found for Carl and me it was a time we could establish a rapport with our children. It was a learning process for not only Carl and I, but for our children. Today, many families do not sit down at the table, but grab food on the run. Families are missing out on the traditional dinner hour environment. There are many changes in our families' daily lives that have altered the traditional course. Some parents have to work long hours going different directions while most children are busy with all sorts of different activities. It causes much confusion and disorder leaving little time for traditional attributes for family quality time. I found the home requires the entire natural gift as *any* business.

Lunch time at our house is as much about razzing mother as eating. Dan and Carl will come in and when they see the dessert, Dan will say, "Boy, Dad, you have been working all morning!"

Carl will respond, "Yah, I've been baking all morning or I baked before I left!"

Dan sometimes will say—he taught me all I know about cooking. "Mr. Food" happens to be on at our lunch time, and Dan tells me he can't understand why I don't pay a close attention so I can make all those fine desserts. Dan eats lunch with his father and me during the week. It is a time we get to visit one-on-one.

During the planting or harvesting season, Dan doesn't stop to get out of the tractor, sprayer or the combine. It would be too time consuming. Carl or I take his lunch to the field. He is able to eat while the combine is going using his GPS.

At our house breakfast, dinner and supper still apply today, for our main meal is at noon time. We eat a lighter evening meal, which works out better for our household.

The children, especially Wil, would leave me notes of a warmth magnitude of their love throughout their growing years. It sometimes was just "I love Mom". I have kept everything. There may be a few things that have gotten away, but not much. It is a fun time to get the boxes out and reminisce—precious memories!

When Dan was seven or eight he started helping me by drying the dishes when Deb wasn't around—and some when she was. It was so helpful; he became a pro! It had never been an assigned chore. Each still do little things that amaze me. Each is good to ask us to go places with them ... out to eat or once-in-a-while the movies. We are so blessed!

During one school year, our granddaughter, Jessica, asks me if I would answer some questions for one of her classes. There were six questions about my definition of *my* American Dream. The first question was: Has your dream changed over the years, and how has it changed?

My answer: *No*—I would like to see the teaching of how to live being less selfish and learn to love and give. We have seemed to heedlessly forgotten. Material things rather than giving help to those who need our strength and assistance are dominating our course. Wealth and progress are good if we don't forget what our American Dream is! We have grown to the point money, power and pleasures serves that dream today. My definition of the American Dream is to believe in human equality with respect to social, political and economic rights and privileges. A prosperous country is marked by a successful economic growth of well-being. What best symbolizes an American Dream, I think, is the use of science to develop and represent logical principles by means of a formalized system. This is my collage of *The American Dream.*

Overall, the most valuable lesson taught should be of positive thinking. Being positive, this makes a world of difference. In children's teaching it is important for them to understand the importance of rationalizing the intersection between responsibility and authority. Good philosophy seems to be: provide children with opportunities and let them learn by trial and error—makes one become their own coach.

As a grandmother, I can say, it is a time of true joy. Children have away of making you forget you are tired. The power of their love that they bestow upon you can be so amazing and warms the heart. With their trusting eyes, smile that wins our heart makes one feel so blessed. They are trusty soles; fearless of danger, but when I look at our children and grandchildren—I know how rich I am—an American Dream of LEGACY! We all have our dreams like the two Christopher's that I have written about. They both gave it a good fight up to the end leaving by showing us all about optimism—an American Dream of HOPE!

Christopher Kennedy brought love and left it for us *all* to remember

~ CHAPTER 14 ~

GUIDING LIGHT OF HOPE

$\mathscr{C}$hristopher Reeve meant *hope*—he had done a lot toward trying to find a means to help those with a spinal cord injuries. One day, there will be a breakthrough for those with such injuries. I read recently where a major step toward that goal may have been achieved at the Miami project to cure paralysis. The researchers say they have found a way to promote the growth of the nerve fibers in damaged spinal cords and prevent post-injury nerve death. The research focused on transplanting cells from peripheral nerves outside the brain and spinal cord into the damaged area as a bridge across the injury.

Cells from adult rats were used. New fibers didn't go beyond the bridge due to problems the research found including growth-inhibiting molecules. A three-part approach was done shortly after the injury occurred.

My close friend was telling me about the breakthrough in

Portugal that she had seen recently on a local TV station. There were 48 surgeries that had been done using stem cells from the patient's nose to implant in the spinal cord. One patient was shown taking a few steps, but still needed extensive therapy. Research has come a long way with much *hope*.

The last research I have read is from our own <u>Purdue University Research.</u> Purdue says they may have isolated the chemical most responsible for tissue damage that follows such traumas. The development of a drug to detoxify that substance could improve treatments for paralysis and other chronic conditions, as Alzheimer's and Parkinson's disease.

Acrolein is produced by the body and benign at normal levels. It becomes hazardous when its concentration increases, as it often does in tissue that experiences stress such as exposure to smoke or pesticides. Acrolein may be the key in causing paralysis after the trauma of a spinal injury. When a spinal cord ruptures, not only are the traumatized cells at increased risk of damage from free radicals that oxidize the tissue, but the cells also spill chemicals that actually help the free radicals to launch repeated attacks. The use of Acrolein has already been implicated in cancer and neurological diseases, so new drugs that detoxify it could become important in treating spinal cord damage.

The research at this time is focusing on recent spinal injures. Science has long been aware that some chemicals that damage cells are part of the problem, but no one has ever been sure which chemicals are responsible. More research will be needed to see if spinal cords that have been injured for sometime could be helped— long has been a question of mine. I choose to have hope.

Physicians have long recommended a diet rich in antioxidants, such as vitamins and C and E—which are able to attach themselves to free radicals, detoxifying them. Antioxidants are important and do help. Statistics show there is a spinal cord injury on an average of every 48 minutes.

As for Christopher Reeves, he and wife, Dana, had been an

inspiration for everyone around the world. As Dan has always said, "You can always look around and see someone worse." How true! Christopher showed us how faith, determination and courage do pay off. His family was there for him which was most significant to Christopher's well-being. Dana had shown so much grace throughout his and her ordeal. They made effective advocates for the disability awareness. Christopher spent the major portion of his time after his injury exploring how he could resolve the difficult issue of a paralytic with commitment and much willingness.

Christopher and Dana Reeve will be truly missed, without them we would not be where we are in Spinal Cord Research today. Young Dana died from cancer and is together again with her beloved Chris. They have left a legacy in death that will pilot the course for the need of stem cell research arguments. Chris not only had the talent but the ability and reason to be persuasive, work his children have chosen to carry forward.

~ CHAPTER 15 ~

OLD HABITS ALONG WITH NEW HELP

*D*an has had different bouts with being in the hospital for bladder infections and has had some blood clots. He has made an exciting breakthrough; It has been a few years for him to be placed in a hospital as a patient. Time helps *to know how* and *what to* or *not to* do. He works cautiously at taking care of his body. With prudent forethought helps to minimize hospital stays.

Dan is so lucky he is able to use his upper body and breathe on his own. Although he is in a wheelchair I am sure there are times Dan puts this brave face on for his family. Dan endures much pain that no one knows about. One cannot imagine what a paralytic goes through. After Dan's injury some would say, "I know what you're going through," but until you have had the experience—one does not know.

I have a dear friend that I can always vent with. Louise Fugate was and is always there for me. She never pretended to understand

119

what the family was going through but would listen and offer technical support or assistance that she may help with.

Carl, like me, was hurting for Dan. All I could do was put my arms around him when he came in and leaned over a back of a chair crying. I never knew what was going through Carl's mind, for he never expressed his feelings verbally—which made it hard for me. Carl is a watcher and listener, not a talker, a quiet person. I tried to be confident. It was so hard to watch you're once lively, vivacious son struggle doing what once had been easy.

I thought—God hath not promised joy without sorrow, peace without pain. Those thoughts helped to change my approach towards the weeks and months that followed with faith.

Dan being so brave never experienced depression for he understood what was ahead for him and chose to meet the facts head-on. He never gave in to self-pity; all it would do was slow up the progress he had achieved so fast. Dan learned to use leg braces for his work on the farm while in physical therapy. It was while in physical therapy he realized he was dependent on others for help. Braces enable him to get into his pickup. If he has something to support him he can stand up, but he wouldn't be able to without his braces. He uses them whenever he is on his equipment or lawn mower. Dan modified his lawn mower, himself, so he can use it.

He is very meticulous with the way his lawn looks. There are a lot of people that compliments on how nice he keeps it. Donya was asked if they had someone to care for it. They have a large lawn, plus, with the roadside he mows around five acres. Dan's a doer, not a grumbler about his life changes. I use to worry with him mowing, for if Dan reaches a distance he will fall forward with him having lack of balance. It still is to a degree a concern. I have never said anything to him, for he would do it anyway....

Dan keeps all his equipment maintained in good shape. He makes it a priority to see that all the equipment has been gone through thoroughly each year. It is costly, but in the long run cheaper for him. Dan is aware the need to keep the maintenance maintained with him being unable to check it himself, plus, the time factor. Parts are not readily picked up today, for the dearlerships don't stock inventory as they once did. Good preventive maintenance helps minimize downtime for which is significant to putting a crop in. Time is of the essence. Dan can plant 20-30 acres of corn and 30 acres of beans in an hour. When the season is over, Dan makes it a mission to see that all the equipment is cleaned and put in the shed. The beauty of living exists in striving. Dan established a work habit early in his youth—habits that last a lifetime.

~ CHAPTER 16 ~

WITH A THANKFUL HEART

*A*fter Dan's injury, rods were put in when they operated to help the vertebrae stay in alignment. They got to hurting so bad Dr. Feuer agreed to operate on Dan to remove the rods himself. Nurses told Dan he didn't normally do that, but for Dan he did. The tender care and concern shown to Dan was something we shall never forget with a thankful heart. Dan was happy that Dr. Feuer was going to do the surgery; he felt comfortable with him.

Carl constructed a mat table for Dan. Dan had a foam pad made and covered with vinyl to fit the mat table. It is firm and enables him to slide and move easier. Covers have to be left loose at the foot of the bed for Dan; it enables him to be able to move. As Dan's body has been disrupted from the spinal cord injury, he requires higher temperature and more covers than most of us do. Sometimes he will be sweating before he can go to sleep. He never says it is too hot; instead it is too cold!

After an injury many insurance companies won't pay for certain things for a patient's need. In today society there are patients that could be helped that are being turned away. One has to rely on self-discipline in caring for themselves or families to keep the body degenerating. Many patients who are chronically ill or injured quickly reach the limit on their health insurance. They are forced to get rid of their assets to qualify for assistance. I really feel for those that don't have a family backing and no funds. One can only wonder—do they get lost in the system? When Dan was in the hospital there were patients you found yourself wishing you could do something to make their lives better. It was hard to have to look and walk away.

Barry Delks the director of breaking New Ground Resource Center at Purdue helped Dan a lot after his spinal cord injury. Purdue's Breaking New Ground Center has become internationally recognized as a source of information on rural assistive technology and strategies for improving services to rural residents with disabilities. The last count known to us there were 19 "AgrAbility" states, and Purdue supports them with resources, technical advice and training. It is truly a gift for the disability to have those like Barry Delks that care.

Dan worked helping to carry the message through doing slide show presentations for the National Farm Machinery Show and 4-H groups. The team members from the Department of Agricultural Engineering were: Bill Fields, and Gary Stoops, outreach coordinator. Mr. Delk's important achievements of Breaking New Ground were many. These three fellows were very helpful to help Dan. It was estimated that more than a million individuals have had direct contact with Breaking New Ground awareness. Words cannot say what these men gave of themselves to help the disabled—may their deeds always be remembered. The former Dean of Agriculture said, "The new award, which recognizes team accomplishments, was established because he believes that inter-disciplinary collaboration is the key to fostering the missions of Purdue Agriculture." "Breaking

New Ground" visited Dan within two weeks after his injury.

"Breaking New Ground" link farmers with new products, fabrication shops and inventions. He was informed about all the constructed equipment available to get him into the equipment himself, and to get around the house. He was introduced to the sources of information and the mechanical aid involved: motorized farm scooters, heavy-duty wheelchairs and lifts.

Former Dean of Agriculture, Victor L. Lechtenberg, is Donya's former boss. He will be missed. Mr. Lechtenberg was recently advanced at Purdue to the position of vice provost of engagement. Barry Delks is with the Animal Science Department at Purdue.

There is a neighbor Richard "Rick" Ward that went to the same school as Wil and Dan. He was a grade between our sons. Rick contributed much to helping Dan. At the time, he was farming with his father; now he does the management since his father's retirement.

Gary Standiford, a special person and friend, had been with Dan most of the day of his injury, but had left shortly before Dan's fall. Gary and wife, Connie, along with Dr. Gilbert (Gil) Gutwein and wife, Mary Jo, came to the hospital that evening as soon as they heard about Dan's injury. We were all in shock with startling fear viewing the situation with alarm for Dan. They stood beside the family in the long vigil waiting. Gary, Connie, Gil and Mary Jo's attentiveness was appreciated and not forgotten.

Gary is a large farmer. Rick Ward farms next to Dan, and Gary has farm ground in the area.

Dan tried using lifts to get into his equipment, but found the designed parts used not readily available. He would have to have the repair parts made making the up keep too expensive to keep the lifts maintained. There is an economic impact of the injured. Dan had lost income potential and also incurred more expenses at the same time. He had accident insurance but he never received any compensation. Insurance companies today have a clause for this or that allowing them not to have to pay. There are people that do abuse their insurance just because they have it; which just compounds the problem.

Most didn't think Dan should continue farming. The number of doubters out-weighed the number of supporters. Some told him direct he had no business farming. As the children were growing they were taught not to be resentful about things. We taught them to pickup and move on. Dan is not resentful and has no remorse ... this I am so thankful for. He says, "The law of averages says there's going to be a certain percentage of people who are disabled and on that day, it was me."

I feel Dan was and is a leader for those around him. Seeing how motivated Dan was after the injury *I believed with all my heart* that Dan *could* and *would* continue farming. I went to bat for him; I would have challenged anyone on that belief. He still had a lot to give! Dan's handicap had not robbed him ... just a new way of doing! As parents, Carl and I are proud of Dan and his stubbornness. Had he listened to outsiders, his story would be a different one today ... depending on others. Courage cannot be taught; it emanates from one's principles, values and one's moral and ethical belief—it takes courage to rebuke as Dan did. Dan on the behalf of the "handicap awareness" has shown infinitely something more powerful than words can say, for he is a winner.

There have been some who have personally reached out as a "connector" to help Dan with a job or just answering a question: Phil McKinsey, for auto electrical needs and Rex Beck, a design engineer with Tipmont REMC. Rex has been helpful with his electrical knowledge in helping Dan with his different grain set-up projects. They are two truly gifted men with so much talent, plus, they have this *special* gift of showing amiable support. Dan will never forget Phil and Rex who, with their help, and with their caring, made life easier for him.

Phil has been there for Dan since he returned to farming in the fall after his injury. Phil McKinsey had an accident in 2005 and laid in a coma for a few days. He has gotten back to work, but still recuperating from the accident. He experienced a lackadaisical sense for awhile, but was gradually returning to his lively, animated character. Phil, a positive person, would learn he had a greater battle to fight. Phil died in 2006 from cancer. He worked right up to the end—what a trooper!

To be a strong and healthy nation, we must have the knowledge and the science. I pray one day we will see more research funding put into place for the many different disabilities that plague our country. It is not realized many don't have the funds for the assistance that they need. Some are tired of trying to get assistance and they just give up. Our soldiers are coming home at this time facing the same situation—many having to fight for their benefits! Their injuries mostly have been caused from explosions—which are catastrophic injuries: burns, multiple amputations and head trauma. I heard a medical team say that 90% of those that have been injured would not have survived just ten years ago. What a giant strive for our country's medical research knowledge.

Dan had insurance; unfortunately he never got a dime. Dan was told he should have sued but he said, "It won't bring back my legs." He chose to move on and decided he'd have to find his own way to get what he needed. To "The Breaking New Ground" team and those like Rick Ward, Phil McKinsey, Rex Beck, Ty Nannet and Gary Standiford—Dan was shown they did CARE for they gave their assistance in helping with an outstretched hand and support. Dan didn't ask for any help and chose to do it his way—on his own with family.

~ CHAPTER 17 ~

WE NEVER WALK ALONE

*A*s the children were growing up I was in the hospital a lot. It was hard on them as well as Carl. It seems things all happen at the same time. Wil had just started the first semester in the sixth grade when he became quiet ill with a kidney infection and rheumatic fever. He missed the whole first semester. I home schooled him. Deb would bring his assignments home each day. Just before Christmas I took Wil to the doctor and he asked the doctor to see why Mother was falling. That day we found I would have to have another surgery. Thank God I had gotten the Christmas shopping all done, which was unusual. It was a good thing for I ended up being away for several weeks. I was sent on soon after surgery to a hospital in Chicago. It was rough being away from home, especially, the children, but I didn't have a choice. I didn't get along after the surgery due to an allergy. The specialist said he was surprised I made the trip. It was a trip I don't remember much about.

Dr. Randolph, the top specialist in the nation in his field at the time said, "You wouldn't be here today if it weren't for Dr. Leak." One of the nurses knew Dr. Leak. She told me that he was ahead of his time when he was in medical school.

Doctor Leak always took a special interest in his patients. There were times after his diagnosis he would say, "Let's get a second opinion to make sure." I never knew him to misdiagnose. He is truly missed since his retirement. He was a doctor that would take time to make a diagram that would help to explain something more clearly … ardently dedicated and loyal; a genius with medical knowledge.

Whenever I was in a local hospital under the care of Dr. Leak or Dr. Gary, my surgeon, the nurses would always ask, "How are you related?"

My response was, "I'm not!"

Their response was, "Hmm! They make sure that you get the best of care."

That was the type of care they each gave throughout all their doctoring me. I admired them and felt safe in their care. Dr. Gary, after a long day of surgery would go home and care for his invalid wife by himself. She was ill for several years. He was a devoted father, husband as well as doctor.

I had lots of allergies; certain foods, very petrolchemical allergic (cannot eat anything with any chemical residues) and allergic to tobacco smoke. Thank God, I never did drink or smoke. I would get hives when I got around a Camel cigarette. I have always had a large garden and do a lot of canning and freezing. That way I don't have to worry what is in this or that. I have a filtered water system. I only drank water, milk, tea, juice and once-in-awhile I will drink a glass of sprite or ginger ale. I do not eat anything out of a store can product other than pineapple. The gold or white on the inside of the cans and lids are lined with preservatives (a chemical compound)… everything is so full of preservatives. When I go to town, there are some places I have to hold my breath and quickly get out of the store. I do a lot of baking and use to make all of the ice cream when the children were home. I have *never* used a box mix for anything. People don't realize today what food taste like without chemicals. Family and friends have been good working with me through the years.

On Christmas Eve of that year, Carl didn't get to bed until around twelve after returning home from the hospital. Deb said it was around two that Wil woke up saying, "Merry Christmas!"

This was no surprise to me! Wil was the one that always got up before the other two on Christmas morning. Dan would always go to bed when he got tired no matter who was around. He would be there and then he would be gone! We would wonder—where is Dan? He'd be in bed. None of the children would sleep in of a morning. They were never hard to get up for school and were always cheerful.

Wil was like me. I never required the sleep that my brothers and sisters did. Mother would always say, "I don't care for you to stay up if you don't bother anyone else." Wil, we handled the same way and it worked out fine. One of those late nights "God's Magnificent Work" was probably written. Deb and I heard him singing and playing the guitar one night, but he never knew we were around. When he was in high school he sang with the "North Montgomery Swing Choir Group" that had won first place in competition, the High School Athletic Department trainer and one of nine high school students chosen to attend the annual Indiana High School Government Leadership Conference.

The conference, sponsored by Indiana Senator Birch Bayh, was sanctioned by the Indiana Secondary School Principals Association. Sen. Birch Bayh, father of our former Indiana Governor and now Senator Evan Bayh.

Wil has a broad interest in many things. He is very good with photo taking and had done weddings while going to Purdue and working at Berry's Camera Shop. He is, also, very talented with making beautiful furniture. He defiantly was a child that put what he learned to its best use. He got to work on a grant project "The Development of Photoreceptor Responses in the Embryonic Chick"; an Honors Degree in the Department of Biological Sciences while at Purdue University. Wil helped with the publication of the Science Newsletter. He found both to be knowledgeable and interesting—something that was challenging. Wil always has had a broad interest. He was always busy doing something.

Carl and little Deb had to carry a large load. We were in the process of moving when I had to go in for surgery. I don't know how they managed. There was so much to do. Our dear friends, Don and Louise Fugate, and son, Bill, helped what they could. There was a lot of growing up for the children in that period in their lives. They missed me as I missed them. It wasn't easy, but I chose to look forward not back.

With the distance I didn't have many visitors, but I did get a lot of cards. Dr. William Sholty, my anesthesiologist, did come to see me. It was such a surprise! We had a good visit. We talked once after I got home. He gave up his anesthesiologist work and became the coroner for his county due to an allergy.

During World War II, Dr. Sholty served with the 104th Evacuation Hospital where he followed General Patton across Europe. Dr. Sholty lived to be 90 years old. Dr. Leak, also, served during the war here in the states. His high IQ placed him with an official job here at home. Those soldiers were needed too. He had had his first year of med-school when he entered the Army. They both have distinguished characteristics and have served their country to the greatest degree. The breadth of their care was reaching out with passion. Dr. Leak never went much on trips due to all the work that would be there when he got back. In later years he took up the sport of skiing and just loved it. He said, "I wish I had started sooner."

While in the Chicago Hospital Carol Channing and Gordon

Palmer were both on the same floor as I was. Carol wasn't too far down the hall from me. We all three had Dr. T. Randolph. Carol Channing was certainly demanding where Gordon was quiet; you never heard anything from him. The nurses sure liked him and thought he was a nice patient. Another patient that was in the next room to me was a young women doctor. She was pretty ill. She would come in to check on me and would hold my hand. We both were lonely and she knew I was missing my family. She was still there when I went home. After so long one loses contact and then after some time has past, you get to thinking about those (as the doctor) that touched your life.

Carl couldn't come to the hospital as he would have liked, but it was just as well for I was so sick at that time it wouldn't have been any need for him to be there and see what I had to go through. It was a two and half-hour drive from home. Carl was needed at home for the children were in school. The children would send me little notes when Carl came on a week day. No words could tell in part what their notes and letters meant to me. It made those long days closer to home. Carl would always try to bring them to see me on weekends. It would have been hard on both the children and me not to see each other. It was always a joy to see their smiles.

There was a young black fellow that worked at the hospital that would go the gift shop and make a list of different things that could be purchased to give or send home for the children. From the list I would make a choice and he would go and purchase my selection. He always looked out for Carl when he came to visit, for the hospital was located in a rough neighborhood. He once told Carl to go move his car to a safer area. He was afraid it would get stripped where he had parked. Carl most of the time would leave before it got dark out.

I had a roommate that was an older lady with a heart condition. She was very nice. I don't think she ever got to go home, for I tried to contact her to no avail. She was disappointed when I was released, for we had gotten along so well. She had become quite fond of my family and Dr. Randolph. She was from the Chicago area.

On my homecoming I noticed some ketchup on the floor; I automatically took a piece of wet toweling and wiped it up. I never thought anything about it, but I think it bothered Deb, for she said, "I had meant to wipe it up and forgot it." I have wished I had not done that for she had worked so hard helping Carl with the daily chores. She tried to have everything just right for my homecoming that she had forgotten about the ketchup. She was so young to have to shoulder what she did. I just didn't think about what I was doing at the time. I had not said anything about it being there. It was so good getting home that I just automatically started to do what I had always done—being *Mummy*! I am and have always been a workaholic.

I was amazed how Carl was able to move with my being in the hospital. There was a lot of work yet to do, but he and Deb had done a superb job—a task that had to have been hard! Everything from then on seem too flow easily, and soon everything was in order.

I suffered from headaches for a while. Upon my homecoming the wind was blowing so hard that when I opened the car door to step out the door blew back and hit me above the left eye. Carl took me to Dr. Leak for fear I had a concussion, but it turned out to be just a nasty blow. There is an indentation in the eyebrow area where I got hit yet to this day. I don't remember why we didn't pull into the garage, but I think I was scheduled for a Doctor's appointment.

Wil was getting better ... Thank God! We had been told he wouldn't be a well boy for a long time. He gradually got stronger. He returned to a new school the second semester. He never missed much school after the one semester. Deb said he did lay on the sofa after school a lot. I am sure he would have as sick as he had been. He was never a complainer. He would read a lot. When he was in the third grade the teacher told us we would have to keep him challenged. She said he would get his work done and would start reading a book.

When he was in the second grade there was a new library put in the elementary grades at the school. Wil was the one that got to introduce it to the parents. When I went for the introduction it was not known that Wil would be introducing the library. I don't think he know it ahead of time either. He did a superb job and was quite elated about the library.

I have a picture of Wil at age three looking at a book while still in bed early one morning. Carl, too, is an avid reader. It is hard to keep him in reading material. When the children were young, the day "Guidepost" came we all would grab for it, except Dan. The one who got their hands on it first would get to read it. Usually it was Carl or Wil. Deb and I just had to wait our turn. Reading has always been a big thing in our house.

Dan was never much to read until he was a little older. He likes the John Grisham books. He has started a collection of books, he, too, has become a reader when time allows. He gets plenty of reading with all the farm business that he has to attends to. He has a lot of bookwork that requires much of his time leaving not a lot of free time. It is a time in history everything calls for paper work—paper work. Farming is a hands-on responsibility, whether it's in marketing, or purchasing.

Dear Mother,

How are you? I sure hope you are feeling well. I miss you so verry, verry ~~much~~ much dear mother. It just doesn't seem right like ther is somthing very important missing and that is you.

I have being getting along in school very well. Mrs. Phillips called and said she was retiring from school and going as a subitute teacher. I was sure surprised to here that. Well, I have to go now. You had better be auful good now good by.

With so ~~very~~ much love

Your Son,
Danny

P. S. I love the pin.

Dan wrote this letter when I was in the hospital in Chicago. He was 9 years old.

CHAPTER 18

HELP YOURSELF TO BRIGHTENED THY CORNER

$\mathcal{D}$an found combating public's view almost as hard as being handicapped. For Dan the four years after his accident he says, "A tough transition period." There is a negative stereotype of the handicapped in society ... sad, but true. It all adds to the coping period.

Dan went into an equipment dealership to buy a tractor. The salesman was unfriendly and wouldn't shake Dan's hand. He didn't seem to take Dan serious about purchasing a tractor. The salesman lost the sales for the owner. My brother, Floyd, found out about it and went to the dealership and talked to them about what happened. The owner told Floyd for Dan to contact him personally. Of course, no boss likes to hear they lost a good sale. Dan did buy a tractor at another dealership.

At a local dealership one day, Dan was reaching for a brochure and a fellow employee was walking by as Dan was about to get it, and the fellow reached over and pushed it back and walked on. He didn't come back in a teasing way to retrieve it for Dan. It was in an area that took some effort for Dan to get it. These types of acts are beyond disbelief. The saying is: children can be the cruelest things on earth—I think that applies to some adults as well. For the most part, dealerships employees are very considerate. Many will and do go out of their way to help Dan. One learns where to go and where not to go. Dan doesn't want to be treated any differently than someone who has no handicap ... just treated with respect!

For several years he volunteered for Breaking New Ground Resource Center at Purdue University (Program for helping Americans with Disabilities), speaking to 4-H groups and did a video for American Farm Safety Week. Dan, as a member of the Purdue Breaking Ground program, did television interviews, served on the board of directors of the Indiana Easter Seal Organization, serves as a board member (past chairman) of the SWCD Montgomery County Soil and Water Conservation and is a current local Westland Co-op Director. The Westland Co-op is now called Ceres Solutions. Three Indiana member-owned cooperatives merged together to form Ceres Solutions, LLP. Dan has worked closely with and respects President and CEO, Jeff Troike, and all of the board members.

The part *Ceres* is a Roman word that denotes agriculture. Ceres was suggested by son, Dan, and is pronounced as "series". *Solutions* was suggested by the management appointees. Dan serves as Ceres Solution's Chairman.

Dan has had to learn to work with adversity. Perseverance has paid off for Dan. He is the type of person that keeps busy. His steadfast action to take things beyond a desired point is something we are so proud of. Self-esteem and discipline helps in providing one's enforcement of achieving. The glass is just half full if you want it to be. Dan doesn't take the "glass half empty" view.

When Dan spoke to the youth groups they would listen intently while he was speaking. They would ask questions and Dan would answer their questions the best he could—children do ask questions! They were always eager to know different things about him being in the wheelchair. He and Donya spoke to a young group together. It wasn't until they were finished that the children were told that Dan and Donya were married.

He used to help with "Ag Day" a farm demonstration for school children. Dan welded reinforcing rods to hold ears of corn to display on front of the corn header of the combine to show the city children how the combine gathers the corn. He talked to implement dealers asking them to furnish equipment to educate the city children about farming and the equipment used. Dan has quit helping, for it was during the fall harvesting; right at his busiest time. He would always respond with a *yes* when ask to speak or help out with something, but he found commitments were hard for him. He has learned to be more selective with working commitments in around his time schedule.

SWCD provides a variety of programs and service to a farmer's resource concerns. He likes and enjoys SWCD and his Westland Co-op board, for they both call for decision making—this he likes! Dan likes to see progress and being on the three boards certainly calls for looking forward to what will better meet the farmers' need. He has found the Westland Co-op board has a utopia visionary goal for an ideally system structure for the farmers it supplies.

Donya always ask Carl and me to go to the Indiana State Fair. She is there every year for the Ag Alumni Association. The first time we went, at the other end of the building where Donya was located, I just happen to see a picture of Dan. While standing there looking at it a fellow told me there was a picture of Dan that had been put on the ceiling of the new Methodist Rehab Center in Indianapolis. He was unaware I was Dan's mother. Later, at the Hand Clinic in Indianapolis I was looking at a book there and came across a picture and story about Dan. It made me proud that his disability may inspire someone else with a disability to go on and achieve their dream too, for that was what Dan has done. Not everyone can accept his injury as Dan. For Dan, it meant staying focused with his eyes wide open on *I will succeed.*

A lot of incredible things have happened to Dan. It would be good if his story reached and helped just one person. It would be another gain! There are many out there that don't have the means or loved ones that will provide emotional and moral support. They have been through a troublesome and frightening time only to find a lonely directed course without the aid or an alliance to help them seek to meet their goals. They don't have the go-ahead sign to reach a valid acceptance to overcome doubt. Convincing is a very hard sale for those who are living in the real reality of fear with no support system.

Trucks being a part of farming was not a harmonious environment for me. I went through a long period extending back to my childhood where I never understood why I never cared for trucks. Carl and Dan knew this. It is unexplainable for now trucks don't bother me in anyway. Many times since, I have wondered about, could it have been a super natural sense of warning—a message from above? I can't imagine that something this big could ever happen without serious, higher-level intervention. As for Dan, he likes and cares for his trucks. He has the three semi-trucks and a triaxle that he uses to haul grain with. His accident has left him with no sequence of physical mental experience with an unpleasant feel of danger. Dan is pretty brave.

Dan has found accessibility gradually improving. In recent years, increased attention has been given with the passing of the U.S. law for the rights for the disabled are helping those with spinal cord injuries or anyone in a wheelchair. There are a lot of buildings Dan cannot get into yet. This will gradually change for spinal cord injures are becoming pretty common in today's society. There are more people in wheelchairs than ever before. Disability is something people do not ask for. When it does happen it is marked for a quick response for promptness in emergency medical care. Keeping as calm as one can better helps everyone. I learned about strength you can get from a close family life, I learned to keep going even in the worst of times. To a certain extent, I've always followed a feeling.

Dan depends on his phone as a substitute for his legs. It seems he is always on the phone. Either he is calling or someone is calling him. For Dan the cellular phone is a time saver. He handles much of his business with calls; it saves many unnecessary trips. It comes in handy in case of emergencies to check with family. They are small and convenient to carry … like a good tool that is hard to do without.

Carl helps Dan around the farm when his expertise is needed. It was a joy to see Dan carry on his father's work once he semi-retired. Carl had to have another Aortic valve replacement in 2000. He had two cardiac arrest and they had to put in an implantable cardioverter defibrillator. Carl is totally dependent on his pacemaker. It was a rough go the first year; now Carl is doing fine and is very active—with all that cooking that Dan says he and his dad does!!

During Carl's last surgery, they put in a pig valve instead of the mechanical valve. He no longer has to take the Coumadin which he is so grateful. Carl had a horrible experience while on Coumadin not only with the constant monitoring or watching his dietary of vitamin K, but he had a trauma where he cut the main artery in his left hand. There was no way I could have gotten to him in time to take him to the hospital, so he put his army medic training to work. He got in his pick-up and drove 9 miles to the nearest hospital driving with the injured hand and holding the injured wrist with his right hand. It was a horrible sight—blood was everywhere. He drove the back roads because of the traffic on the highway. He chose the back way for he knew there was a chance of his passing out and he felt there would be a less chance of someone else getting injured. Carl was left with a strong power from above helping at the wheel whether he made it or not to the hospital.

After Dr. Leak retired our daughter, Deb, says to her father and me that we should try a local Dr. Brett Spencer. She said, "He reminds me so much of Dr. Leak in his caring for his patients." We took her up on her sound advice, and found him to be as she had described. We love his sense of humor. He has a good staff, nurse and nurse practitioner that are a pleasure to work with. He has been there with us through some rough times just as Dr. Leak had.

Deb had gotten to know Dr. Spencer through her work as Director of Pharmacy at a local hospital. He was a doctor that would use Deb's knowledge as a Clinical Pharmacist. She had been the consultant for the "Athens Medical Specialist" facility that Dr. Spencer had much of the input with establishing.

In 2005, I met the most interesting doctor; Dr. Daniel Gomes, D.D.S., M.S.D. with much of the same characteristics as Dr. Randolph. I had a tooth implant and some gum grafting that he took care of, which all had stemmed from an early youth car accident.

There is something about Dr. Gomes that draws you in and you feel at ease. A very dedicated person; young Dr. Gomes is from Venezuela, South America. He says, "I am *old fashion* in my caring for my patients." What a gift for us patients!

Chapter 19

Reaching Thy Goal, Step-by-Step

*O*ur family has always been very active. We built two of our houses ourselves as well as Carl has done a lot of building type work. The second house we built he told me that I would have to do the plans, for he had done the first one. With my blue prints, Carl built to my designed specifications.

In the late 70's we bought a beautiful house that was 74 years old that took us three years to restore. The boys were well educated not with just farm work but introduced to different types of contract work. Carl used to have a construction business and at one time worked ahead of Morris-Holey highway construction with his equipment. He also did tile ditching putting in farm tile. The farm work was his first enjoyment.

Dan and Donya spent a good while remodeling their home. Dan drew up the blue prints of what he wanted to redo. He hired some help along with using his hired men and his father's knowledge.

It took sometime for them to get to the place it was half livable. I know what they went through for I have been there. It gets to be a pretty trying time to remodel and try to live in the house at the same time. I am sure Donya as well as Dan got to thinking—when will it ever end! There is always something that develops to detour the progress. Remodeling calls for the capacity of much *patience.*

Shortly before Dan's injury, he designed a grain system for Gary Standiford which included converting 6 harvest silos. He put in two grain legs and an automatic drying system. Gary has a large grain facility. Almost all of the grain facilities on farms today are commercialized. Dan has been redoing his own grain handling system to increase the drying capacity and storage.

Capitalizing on storage and timing are everything for today's farmer. It involves committing your thoughts to a design plan. Dan made a trip to Decatur, Indiana about his grain system. Dan had drafted out his plans and when the fellow saw it he said, "I see you have done your homework!"

Dan always makes drafts of any new project. Drafting has always been an interest of Dan's. I am surprised he didn't major in it when he was going to Purdue. His plan to return to the farm may have had something to do with his chosen major. After Dan was injured he returned to Purdue to get his master's degree, but with his therapy and the farm work it all got to be too much.

When Dan was in grade school I would notice my discarded boxes would disappear from the trash. One day, I found it was Dan that was retrieving them. The oatmeal boxes he would create grain bins; making a grain system facility. He was my "recycle" kid! He spent hours adapting my "throw away" to a new use with his natural ability to create. He painted the oatmeal boxes a silver color and made the down spouts out of straws. He still has those creations. Those creations have become indispensable for his purpose of carrying out plans today. One time, he modified some of his tractors and redid a toy dozer. He received a good scolding, for his project called for him using parts from Wil's toy tractor.

The tractor was a replica of the first new John Deere tractor Carl bought. Both boys had been given a replica at the time of Carl's purchase.

It was through the origin of work-activities: body, mind and machine that Dan found much strength and direction to overcome the barriers to succeed. As making clothes on my trusty Singer sewing machine was always a comfort zone for me. In work or keeping busy with something constructive does so much to open a wider world for challenges. Dan gulped life, and has savored it with a strong will. He is a person that makes me think of the early "John Deere Steel Plow" that scoured brightly into the soil. Dan would scour his *dream* working as hard as the plow had to work choking into the foulest of ground. His dream made his task easier and helped to open vast ideas to success as the plow for our early settlers.

Today Dan farms around 2,450 acres. He has fulfilled his dream! It takes determination and lots of will power—that Dan has! It was and is still astounding to his father and me what Dan is able to do. He has never wavered from his goal and I feel he has met it by not looking for the things he *can't* do, but looking for what he *can* do. There are times life overwhelms us that is when one should stop to remember, we are not alone, for God holds the key to the future. It is sometimes hard when our lives have emphasis focusing in so many directions. One has to keep reaching for a goal despite any limitation one has—believe in tomorrow! It is much more satisfying looking forward to I can rather than to I can't. One has to practice their mission to reach their goal by actively engaging in a specified course of action. It is more intelligent to hope rather than to fear, to try rather than not to try using every opportunity to advance your goal.

If it weren't for the wheelchair one wouldn't know Dan is paralyzed the way he handles himself. One day there was a fellow looking for us and had stopped at Dan's house. He had seen the Pioneer Seed dealer sign that Dan has up with his name on it. Dan was on his scooter and the fellow followed him down to the shop. In the loose gravel Dan got stuck and he asks the fellow, "Would you, please, give me a push?"

The fellow responded, "Are you disabled or something?"

It is amusing for Dan to tell for there is no way he would have been on a scooter otherwise. It is good that he can laugh in the light of his situation.

I learned long ago that the best way to finesse a difficult problem is stay true to oneself. I knew as a young child growing up to be a time of hardship; nowadays, things are much different for children. When I look to Dan's early beginnings, I see this little boy that his father and I tried to give a firm foundation on which he could build a predictable and dependable existence. I never realized he was to be challenged by a more difficult path. He has had the courage to choose that path, even in the mist of much despair and uncertainty. I have never seen Dan skeptical for his future since the accident. His experiences, even painful at times, provide answers to questions about our existence, the purpose of life as it may be with sorrow and fear. Dan has had to explore more deeply what succeeding is. He relentlessly lives not showing doubt or skepticism to those around him. He just takes each day with a smile, which will always lighten up my heart!

There is no doubt that those around him have grown in the process—a depth of belief. Dan chose a path with a personal faith, made awareness of a paralytic—life is never to be lightly sacrificed. As Dan told his father after the accident—God has a purpose!

There is in Dan a model of human existence to be perhaps emulated from his traits that are so natural for us all to see. Dan's injury was a blow, but as a family we all did what was best for Dan by holding together. It requires a capacity to readjust endlessly to the changes one has to deal with. It made me pause at times and wonder—how does he stay so brave?

Sometimes the sorrow for Dan was overpowering with the heart crying; there were tears everyday. One has to learn from the situation you are in. Ultimately, we found the ability to face the uncertainties with equanimity. We never succumb to despair, for we knew Dan was not through. Life is not perfect. It wasn't before and it won't be now. One has to consider each day as another day of life a gift from God to be enjoyed as fully as possible.

For Dan there would be a tomorrow, another chance to make a new beginning to what could have been farewell to farming. What a new beginning it turned out to be! Early, Dan accepted the challenge and took action by focusing toward self-discovery and found a reservoir of power to guide him throughout both the troubling and disappointing times. He looked to the foreseeable future as bright and has surmounted his situation with faith each step of the way despite the obstacles.

One shares the knowledge of God's comfort, presence with others who might be suffering. I knew God was with Dan and would guide the way … I believe God works his miracles in many ways. He is there for us if we let him in.

It was not easy for me to write about Dan's accident. But as I began writing from a short story I had written down, in which I had recorded experiences. It brought back a rush of memories, some that were painful and some that made me smile.

It has been a stimulating journey of challenges for our son. Today, I feel wrapped in love, how fortunate one can be with all the ways our family has been blessed? From Dan, the family derived much strength, I was taught to absorb guidance in away I never expected. Dan looked at his beliefs and worked to bring them to light; he had to have been filled with worry, but stayed strong and proud.

Dan's unique smile has away of drawing you in. In it you can see a ubiquitous light showing peace from within, inspiring others to fight apathy—*never giving up.*

> *Thou wilt show me the path of life; in*
> *thy presence is fullness of joy; at*
> *thy right hand there are pleasures for*
> *evermore.*
>
> *(Psalm 16:11)*